FORMULA MARKETING

SUCCESS MADE SIMPLE

DAVID WILKEY

iUniverse, Inc.
NEW YORK   BLOOMINGTON

Formula Marketing
Success Made Simple

iUniverse books may be ordered through booksellers or by contacting:

iUniverse
1663 Liberty Drive
Bloomington, IN 47403
www.iuniverse.com
1-800-Authors (1-800-288-4677)

ISBN: 978-1-4502-5924-8 (sc)
ISBN: 978-1-4502-5925-5 (ebk)

Printed in the United States of America

iUniverse rev. date: 11/5/2010

For Holly with Love

The Great Commission still stands as the most successful marketing campaign in human history.

"Therefore, go and make disciples of all nations, baptizing them in the name of the Father and of the Son and of the Holy Spirit, and teaching them to obey everything that I have commanded you. And surely I am with you always, to the very end of the age."

Matthew 28:19-20

CONTENTS

CHAPTER 1 -
MARKETING: MASTERING THE MATRIX

The marketing department can be the most complicated and potentially expensive department within your company. Mastering the complexities of the marketing matrix is very difficult for a single individual, or even a whole department. You simply cannot be an expert in every discipline of marketing, and the price of not knowing something can cost your organization a fortune.

As a marketing professional, you need to know how to write a newsletter, build a website, design a brochure, follow the moves of your competition, design a tradeshow booth, buy advertising, develop a direct mail list, execute an SEO strategy, stage a photo shoot, write copy, know your customers thoughts and feelings, have a thorough knowledge of your industry, know how to write a press release, understand social media marketing, form strategic partnerships, write a marketing plan, create direct mail campaigns that work, grasp the subtleties of creating a promotion, plan your company conventions and parties, create and maintain a marketing calendar, write a compelling offer, and maintain critical relationships with your clients. Whew! And any marketing professional reading this paragraph knows there is a great deal more to it than the list above.

This is why the marketing department is the busiest department within the company throughout the year. I'll confess that the accounting department is busier at month end and year end – but marketing is ALWAYS busy. As a marketing professional, your work is never finished. If it is, you are not doing your job. There are always marketing opportunities under every rock, around every corner, and with virtually every organization that you meet.

So it is easy to see why many companies and organizations simply do not embrace marketing as a core strategy for building their business and reaching their goals. It is thought to be too time-consuming, too expensive and too complicated. Many companies wave the white flag and surrender.

As an alternative to developing their marketing strategies, many companies simply rely on direct sales. Sales are easy to track – they either happen or they don't. You can simply count up the sales by staff member to determine who is successful and who is not. CEOs and corporate boards understand sales. CFOs and financial staffs understand sales. Even customers understand sales. As a result, sales departments command the lion share of resources, while marketing is often given the scraps. Everyone understands sales, while few people truly grasp marketing. So, why bother with it?

I have worked in and with marketing departments for over 25 years. As an ad agency peon, VP of marketing, sales professional, business development director, business owner, and marketing consultant, I have seen marketing in its many forms. In my experience, the vast majority of companies and organizations do not understand marketing. I further believe that only a small percentage of companies have a marketing plan. Fewer have a dedicated marketing budget, and only a tiny percentage have a coordinated approach to marketing. These organizations may have a marketing department, or a marketing person (many companies will elevate an office manager or sales rep to handle marketing, as part of their job responsibilities), but they do not fully understand the role of marketing for their company. They may believe they should have a marketing department to be successful, but they have not thought through the reasons why.

For me, the most joyful scene to witness in the business world is a company that fully understands marketing. These companies are rare, so they always get my attention. They are like lightning in Southern California. You see it every once in a while, and when you do, you immediately stop what you are doing to watch the show. In fact, I believe lightning is more common.

How can you tell when a company "gets" marketing? These companies exhibit their marketing acumen in a many ways. Here are a few examples:

- They have people on staff dedicated to the marketing matrix.
- They have a marketing plan and a defined budget.
- They have all of their marketing programs working together in concert.
- They have a well established corporate brand and image that are consistent with their marketing plan and initiatives.
- They carefully track the results of each marketing program.
- They record these results and then make controlled adjustments to their campaigns to test different offers, approaches, text, images, timing and designs.
- They carefully refine their programs and they have a good statistical prediction of their expected results before they launch.
- They are consistent with their messaging and their campaigns.
- They periodically add something new to their well-honed marketing matrix to test if better results reside in a different approach or vehicle.

- When they spend money on an initiative, they view it as an investment, rather than an expense.
- They are delighted when a campaign fails, because they have an opportunity to learn from it and not do the same thing again – but they will continue to do the same thing again to make absolutely certain that it does not work.
- They are confident.
- They know their business inside and out.
- The industry knows them, or their company, to be an expert in their field.
- They have a proven marketing formula.

That's the core of it. They have a formula.

The title of this book is the key to successful marketing. To be successful at marketing, you must have a marketing formula. Not a recipe – because many meals can still taste fantastic when you make changes to the recipe. You add a few new ingredients and the meal is often improved. Substitute sugar when you run out of oregano. Just add a dash of teriyaki sauce, a cup of red wine, and you have a delicious new creation. (Clearly this is not a cook book!)

While exciting and creative, the emotionally driven "recipe" approach to marketing will become very expensive over time, with diminishing returns. When asked why these companies elected to change the recipe, I often hear answers like:

- "I have a friend that owns this company…"
- "I love sports and I thought it would be fun to sponsor…."
- "We had a few dollars left over in the budget, so we thought why not…."
- "I have tried everything else and it didn't work…."

And so on.

A marketing formula is precise. It is coordinated. It has no emotion. It has a defined cost. It is a science project with defined objectives, a control group, a hypothesis, carefully recorded results, and an outcome. Successful marketing must have a formula.

In order to lay the foundation of your marketing formula, you will need to have the following in place:

- **Designated Marketing Person or People**
- **Marketing Plan** (aligned with the corporate image & objectives)
- **Marketing Calendar** (developed to execute the plan consistently)
- **Marketing Budget** (based on the calendar and selected tactics)
- **Corporate Consensus** (to follow the marketing plan consistently)
- **Metrics** (to track the effectiveness of the Marketing Plan)
- **Assessment** (to make adjustments as dictated by the metrics)

Does this sound complicated? Are you ready to sell this book at your next garage sale? Before you slap on the 25 cent price tag, let me assure you that formula marketing is simple to learn, and easy to implement. The pages ahead will show you how to write your marketing formula. And once your marketing formula is written, you will just need to adjust it, test it, and maintain it.

The crazy days of flying by the seat of your pants, trying hundreds of different things with the same unpredictable results will be over. Formula marketing is like setting up a bank account and creating the secret code for your ATM card. When you slide your ATM card through the slot, punch in your code and press the correct buttons, a specific amount of money comes out. That's formula marketing. And mastering formula marketing is the mission of this book.

CHAPTER 2:
AUTHORITY & EXPECTATIONS

Your marketing department should not just appear as an expense line on your P&L. Rather, you should have high expectations of your marketing team to provide a handsome return on the allocated budget. The marketing department should be held accountable for their expenditures and their results. All of the marketing programs must generate revenue greater than the related expense of that activity.

When a marketing initiative fails, the reasons must be clearly understood and documented. Meanwhile, the success of other marketing efforts must also be fully understood, refined, and implemented consistently. The rationale for each marketing decision must be consistent with the marketing plan, the corporate brand, and the core demographic of your customers. The results must be provided to the corporate stake holders – I am talking about proving your results with colorful graphs, financial spreadsheets, statistical data, and customer surveys.

Does this sound unfair? Would your marketing team quit or be fired if they were held to these standards? Wait just a minute. I am not finished. These expectations are reciprocal. Let me explain.

I believe that the most common reason why companies fail with their marketing plans is that ownership or management does not fully support the decisions of the marketing department. When cash flow is tight, they cut the marketing budget. When a program does not yield the expected results, they want to make a change. Someone in management will have a flash of insight and want to add a new twist to the marketing plan.

Interference with the marketing department happens all the time. It is, I believe, one of the most destructive forces in the business world. Interfering with the marketing department is like blindfolding a pilot minutes before landing, or changing the script halfway through a Broadway production. However, it happens in every organization. But why?

The answer is simple. Marketing is fun. That's where the action is for most organizations. The marketing people throw the parties, create the designs, receive the corporate perks, and launch the campaigns. Their offices and cubicles are filled with color, creativity, and life. Creative ideas bounce off the walls, new concepts fly across the room, and something is always happening.

The accounting department is just not that exciting. Rarely does a manager from another department walk into accounting or finance and said "Hey, I have a creative idea for our year end financials!"

Sales, while often linked with marketing, is dull and predictable by comparison. Production offers many opportunities for creativity, but it is not nearly as dynamic as marketing. The operations department is the core of the business, but the procedures and policies don't hold a candle to the creation of new corporate tag line. And the list goes on.

For this reason, people will often want to visit marketing, offer their ideas, and make changes. Company owners and presidents are famous for this. Everyone has an opinion about marketing.

As a result, many marketing departments are forced to add ideas from the field (a dash of teriyaki sauce), incorporate new programs from the sales department (a cup of wine), and include the flash of insight from the president's spouse (substitute sugar for oregano). While these contributors are smart, gifted people with important opinions, their interference in the marketing department will, in most cases, result in a watered down recipe, higher expenses and declining results. However, the greatest calamity from this interference is that the marketing formula is not followed. Sometimes mistakes in the lab lead to a cure (like the discovery of penicillin), but generally this kind of interference serves to ensure that a cure is never found.

So, as we discussed, the strict expectations and demands placed on marketing must be balanced with equal adherence to the marketing formula. This means that interference with the marketing plan cannot be tolerated. Interference comes in many forms. Here are a few of the most common:

Cutting the Marketing Budget: You must set your budget for a given term that matches the marketing plan and stick to it. No exceptions. Make contingency plans to avoid cutting the budget from marketing. The fact is, marketing is usually the first thing cut when a company fails to meet forecasts or key objectives. However, and everyone reading this book should be aware of this, marketing should be the last thing to be cut in difficult times. Marketing must be viewed as an investment, rather than an expense. However, this is only true when a formula approach is used in your marketing department.

Idea Implementation: Ideas are the lifeblood of every company. I have personally seen terrific ideas come from accounting, customer service, and production. That's not my point. New ideas must be added to the marketing formula at the right time, in the right way. You may need to wait until the end of the fiscal year, or for the next selling cycle, to include these new ideas. A process for evaluating new ideas must be created and governed solely by the marketing department.

Changing the Org Chart: When people change responsibilities within a company, or when new staff are hired, it will often result in interference with the marketing plan. Change within an organization is constant, but the marketing formula must not change, until the appropriate time and for the right reasons.

In summary, marketing departments should be held accountable, but left alone to carry out their plans. Marketing must produce a positive return on investment, with their results clearly documented. If the marketing plan does not produce the expected results, then consider making changes to your marketing staff. That's right. Fire them. However, this can only be done if marketing is given complete control over their area of responsibility. You must set the marketing department free.

Turning Your Marketing Department into a Source of Revenue:

Now that you have given complete freedom to your marketing department, they must produce revenue greater than their expenses. How is this done? Metrics.

All marketing activities must be tied directly to company sales. The relationship of marketing to every sale must be tracked and clearly understood. The sales need to be dissected, to prove what aspect of the marketing plan drove the specific sale. The size of the transaction must be understood, the incremental sales, the total value of the relationship, what products and services are selling. All of this must be connected directly to marketing. But how do you do this? The answer is simple.

Metrics.

CHAPTER 3:
MARKETING METRICS

Formula marketing must produce an outcome that can be tracked. You need a score card that tells you how you are doing with every aspect of your marketing matrix. The numbers don't lie, but people do – or at least they exaggerate.

I am a very optimistic person. I often believe that a campaign will be successful and I am excited about the potential from the initial results. It is not within my nature to lie or exaggerate. I usually see the glass as half full, rather than half empty. This trait often gets me into trouble with my clients, as they could believe that I am over-promising and under delivering. So I am quick to explain to every new client that metrics will be developed for everything we do for them. The metrics will be the method by which they can evaluate the performance of their marketing plan. The numbers will provide the score.

What do I mean by marketing metrics? Metrics are the numbers or values that are produced and tracked to show you how your campaigns are performing. The list below provides some examples:

Marketing Tactic and Resulting Metrics:

Website: Number of Hits
E-Blast Campaign: Open Rate / Number of Click-Thrus
Direct Mail Campaign: Number of Calls & Number of Hits to Designated Landing Page
Special Offers: Number of Coupons Redeemed
Web Advertising: Number of Leads / Sales Tracked to Site
Tradeshow: Number of Leads / Visits to Booth / Appointments Scheduled
Cross-Selling Promotion: Average Ticket Per Customer / Sales

The list provides just a few examples of marketing metrics. Once generated, these values can be tracked, graphed and studied. Once you have good data on each aspect of your marketing plan, you can begin to make subtle refinements and improve your results through them.

I have found that once you begin to generate numbers, you can become obsessed with them. It is not the numbers themselves that drives the obsession, but watching your company moving the needle upward towards greater success. The tricky part of creating marketing metrics is figuring out how you can track each initiative.

Within this chapter, I will provide examples of how to track different areas of your marketing plan. Unfortunately, I will not be able to provide a tracking mechanism for every available marketing vehicle – it would make for a very long book. However, I will discuss the most common ways to create marketing metrics and then allow you to use these ideas to implement metrics within each of your marketing tactics.

Tracking Website Activity: It is critical to have a website in today's business world. I will discuss some of the key elements for developing your website in a later chapter. The point I want to make here is that you must track the hits on, or visits to your website. Beyond hits, it is best to create your website in such a way that you can determine how customers act when they visit your website. What travel sequence do they follow, what pages do they most often visit, what buttons do they click, what forms will they complete and what web-based tools will they use?

Tracking hits is easy to do. However, if you provide your website in all of your advertising, business cards, trucks, and business stationery, you will never be able to determine how these visitors found you. Knowing how they know you is a critical marketing metric.

I suggest creating separate landing pages for your main marketing programs. Landing pages are very inexpensive to create and provide important statistics for your business marketing. Some companies literally have hundreds of landing pages to facilitate tracking their metrics for each marketing initiative. Each of the landing pages will look identical to your website home page and will function in the same, or in a similar fashion. However, your customers will arrive at your website using different addresses.

For example, you should have separate landing pages for each of your advertising channels, vehicles, direct mail, e-blasts, and marketing collateral. Then track the results for each landing page on a monthly basis and record the results. An example follows:

Hits Tracked to Landing Pages

Marketing Vehicle & Hits per Month:
Direct Mail: 435 in January / 722 in February / 677 in March / 546 in April
E-Blasts: 356 in January / 245 in February / 278 in March / 345 in April
Internet Advertising: 316 in January / 298 in February / 312 in March / 289 in April
Magazine Ads: 94 in January / 89 in February / 78 in March / 43 in April

Radio Ads: 56 in January / 34 in February / 49 in March / 51 in April
Truck Signs: 56 in January / 34 in February / 49 in March / 51 in April
Brochures: 89 in January / 67 in February / 55 in March / 49 in April
Promotional Items: 9 in January / 6 in February / 5 in March / 8 in April

Your website metrics will not be perfect. Not every lead will be assigned correctly. Some customers may hear a radio commercial, which reminds them of the direct mail piece they have been holding in their desk drawer. They won't write the website down while driving, but will visit your website through your direct mail piece. So the direct mail piece will receive the credit, but the radio advertisement deserves recognition, too.

Keep this in mind as you evaluate each marketing vehicle. It is often your marketing matrix working in concert that drives your results.

Many companies ask "How did you hear about us?" While this is an important question and must be included within your marketing plan, it is a flawed method for tracking your results. Often the customers cannot remember how they learned of you. Taking the example above, this customer received a direct mail piece, heard a radio commercial, saw you at a trade show, and then used the direct mail piece to visit the website site. When asked how she learned about your company, she may reply "From your website", which may give your SEO investment all of the credit, when the other vehicles contributed to the lead.

Tracking Opt-ins: In a perfect world, you will have the e-mail address of every one of your clients, prospects, and target customers. Building your database of e-mail addresses is extremely difficult and takes time. One of the best ways to build your e-mail database quickly is by offering an incentive on your website for your target customers to "opt-in", meaning they are agreeing to receive more information from your company via e-mail. As part of the opt-in process, these customers will provide you with their e-mail address. In addition to tracking the number of hits to your website, tracking the actions these visitors take is equally important. Opt-in, surveys, forms, orders and direct replies are all tracking triggers that can reside on your website and it is very important to develop mechanisms for tracking each of them.

Examples of Opt-In offers and their results follow:

Opt-In Offer and # of Opt-Ins:

"Join Our E-Club": 2,367
"Join Our VIP Club to Receive Special Discounts": 4,809
"Click Here to Receive our Monthly E-Newsletter": 43
"Click Here to Receive a Free How To Guide": 157
"Click Here to Receive our New Catalog": 1,123
"Click Here to Receive your Invitation to a Free Seminar": 5

"Click Here to Receive a Free Sample": 543
"Click Here to Receive a Special Report": 27

Once the visitor clicks the offer button, a short form field or survey can appear. The visitor then fills in the fields so the item offered can be sent to them. The visitor's e-mail address should always be one of these fields.

If the visitor fills in the e-mail field, they are "Opting-In" to receive e-mails from you. Of course, you will want to track the number of opt-ins you are receiving, based on the current offer. Continue to change your offers and track the results of each. At the end of a given period of time, once you have tested several offers, you will have data on the effectiveness of each offer and can then feature the most successful ones. Continue to make refinements to your offers, so you can adapt to changes within the marketplace. If your opt-in numbers begin to decline, then change the offer. This is one of those projects that will never be finished. You must continue to change and adjust your offers (this is true for all of your marketing activities) while constantly tracking your results.

Tracking Click-Thrus: Once you have a database of e-mail addresses, you can begin to develop and implement e-blast and e-mail campaigns to your target customers. E-blasts and e-mail campaigns are extremely cost-effective, which makes them highly sustainable marketing initiatives and, therefore, an important part of your marketing formula.

Ideally, you have built your own database of e-mail addresses for your target customers. You can add to this list by acquiring additional e-mail addresses or speed-up this process by purchasing e-mail addresses. However, if you purchase e-mail addresses, special care must be taken in segmenting your "purchased" e-mail addresses from your "current customer" e-mail addresses. You can track the success of your campaigns to these two groups by offering different offers to each list.

If you elect to purchase an e-mail list, be very careful to define your target customer and invest in targeting the acquired list to your current customer profile. (We will discuss the importance of defining your target customer in the next chapter, as it is a key component to Formula Marketing.) The business of buying and selling e-mail addresses is growing. These "commercial" e-mail addresses are gathered and sold via sophisticated and widespread "opt-in" third party offer programs. You are able to purchase them from most mailing list and database brokers. However, it is still a new frontier and often these lists are quickly developed and poorly targeted. As a consequence, your results may vary widely from list to list. So be sure to ask plenty of questions regarding how the list was put together and where the e-mail addresses came from.

Once you have your e-mail campaign in place, be sure to install actions within each outbound element of your campaign that allow you to track the actions of the recipients. Once again, you can provide offers to your target customers that they can click. Each of these clicks can then be tracked. You will want to continue to change your offers in the same manner that we discussed in the previous section. While you can use the same form of offers provided for "Opt-Ins", additional examples of Click-Thru offers and tracking follow:

Click-Thru Offer & Number of Click-Thrus:

"Visit our Website": 3,502
"Learn More About Our Company": 341
"Click Here to Receive our Testimonial Packet": 23
"Click Here to Receive a Free On-line Catalog": 457
"Calculate Your Savings" (link to Financial Calculator): 209
"Sign Up Today": 54
"Yes, I would like to Receive a Free Sample": 267
"Click here to receive our latest product White Paper": 71

Tracking Number of Calls: There are generally three main "calls to action" within a direct mail campaign or e-blast campaign:

- Visit our Location
- Visit our Website
- Give us a Call

We have already covered tracking your website hits and we will be sure to cover tracking visits to your location(s), as both are critical metrics for your marketing formula. Tracking your in-bound calls is equally important.

Most companies will track their in-bound calls by having their receptionist ask "How did you hear about us?" While this will give you some good data, it is critical that a tracking program is handled by a defined process without gaps. What happens when the receptionist goes to lunch? What happens when the office is closed? What happens during vacations and holidays? All of these gaps add up to flawed data. Additionally, human error can change the data.

The best way to track your in-bound calls is to track them electronically. Whether you set up a special "customer phone number" that you use exclusively in all of your advertising so you can track the in-bound calls from each campaign (the phone company can provide tracking reports, or you can simply review the phone bill). However, I believe that the best way to track your advertising calls is through designated call tracking numbers.

Companies like CallSource (www.callsource.com) will provide you with a designated number for tracking your advertising calls. These reports are very sophisticated and offer options to record in-bound calls, web-based tracking reports to review the number of calls on a given campaign, the addresses and identities of the customers calling in, as well as some data analytics on who these customers are. All of this data can be carefully tracked and studied to assist you in improving your marketing formula. There are hundreds of call tracking companies in the marketplace. A quick search of the Internet will yield many names. Then visit their website to review their on-line demonstrations to see how these products work. Most of these services are very reasonably priced (approximately $30 per month for a single line). Additional numbers can be added, so you can evaluate the effectiveness of each advertising vehicle (magazine, radio, cable, etc…) and the appeal and effectiveness of each offer.

Tracking Visits - Coupons Redeemed: Tracking visits to your locations, whether retail, restaurant, warehouse, or events is critical to Formula Marketing. Once again, you can ask your customers "How did you find us?" when they enter your location, but there will be significant gaps in the data. Many businesses force this question to be answered at the register – which is fine. But know going in that there will be gaps in your data. However, it will still provide you with some anecdotal evidence for your marketing campaigns.

You can tell I have a bias, just as I do with call tracking. The best way to track your visitors is with redeemed offers. Not only will you learn where your customers are coming from, you will know which offers resonate most with them. Additionally, you can use the questions at the register to learn more about your customers; like asking them to fill out a 3-question survey to receive an additional 10% off. You then keep the coupons, the surveys, and copies of the sales receipts stapled together. At the end of each day, add up the coupons redeemed, add up the sales generated and tabulate your survey results. There are other ways to maximize the sales within each visit to your location. A few follow:

Cross-Sell & Up-Sell: The best way to track the metrics for your up-selling and cross-selling efforts is by tracking your average ticket per customer (the amount each customer spends during a visit). Begin tracking this number and, ideally, track your sales for every category within your business. Developing a simple chart with the monthly sales for each product category, average ticket per customer, and the total sales for the month, will give you a good starting point for your tracking chart.

Then launch your cross-selling and up-selling campaigns and track your average ticket per customer each day, paying special attention to those items that are part of your cross-sell and up-sell programs. Many years ago, I worked for a retail company with several locations across the nation. We began tracking the average ticket per customer. When we started, it was $7.50, with the average location having 150 customers per day. We launched a formal cross-selling and up-selling program and watched the average ticket per customer double to $15.00. Over time, it grew to $25.20 (adjusted for inflation). These programs work, but they require adjustments and consistent training.

Within this company, we tracked the average ticket per customer for every location. We also tracked the sales by category for each location, so we could compare each location with the high and average for each category in other locations. These numbers were very powerful when we evaluated the success of a location. We could then adjust the up-selling and cross-selling programs for a given location to focus on those areas that were below average. Keep in mind, we more than tripled the sales per average location with the same number of customers. This is a big deal, as it translated directly to the bottom line. However, this success would not have been possible if we were not diligent in tracking the key metrics that drove the program.

Up-Selling Defined: Up-selling occurs when the customer is sold a similar item at a higher price. You can witness this on the floor of most car dealerships. Up-selling customers to the more expensive model, with the leather package and the alloy wheels are part of the standard up-sell formula. McDonald's deftly uses their "Super Size It" strategy to up-sell their restaurant customers into a more expensive meal.

Cross-Selling Defined: Cross-selling is a little different from up-selling, in that you are suggesting the sale of an item that is related to the core transaction, but different from the actual item being purchased. For example, when you buy a new winter coat, the sales person may cross-sell you a scarf, hat, and gloves to go with it. Cross-selling happens often in restaurants when a customer buys an entrée, and the server enhances their meal by cross-selling them dessert. The classic example occurs when you visit McDonalds. You are always asked, "Would you like fries with that?" This simple question makes McDonald's one of the largest consumers of potatoes products in the world. Cross-selling is extremely powerful. You just need to determine what the "French Fries" are for your business, or for each core product within your business.

To develop your strategies for up-selling and cross-selling, I suggest that you have a brainstorming session with your staff. Be sure to include the people who actually interact with the customers. They know best the additional items that can be sold to your clientele at the point of purchase. They will suggest items that you had not thought about – in fact, encourage them to suggest things that you don't currently carry. Then, with them leading the meeting, develop an incentive chart.

You may already have an up-selling and cross-selling program in place. Terrific! But does it have a formula? Are you tracking the metrics? Do you know your results across the whole organization? Is the implementation consistent? If not, begin to create the formula for this program.

Once you have metrics in place, you are able to develop a program that provides bonuses to your employees who are successful selling these extra items. The bonus program will drive better results, which you can then implement system-wide.

When it comes to determining your bonus programs, be sure to involve your staff. They must be involved in the program's creation, understand the procedures, be highly motivated by the bonus, and clearly understand how to earn the bonus. If you do these things, you will gain your employees buy-in to the program. However, you cannot give total control of the program to your employees. While you allow them to shape the offers and develop the procedures, management must determine the dollar amounts of the bonuses.

The most important metric to track in this program is not the number of desserts or gloves you have sold, but the average ticket per customer. This is where the bulk of the bonus should be offered. Have your team set an audacious goal. If your average ticket per customer is at $35 now, try to double it to $70. You will be amazed at what your team can accomplish. And these internal selling strategies cost very little money when compared to the cost of other marketing initiatives.

Surveys: When customers visit your location, this is a terrific opportunity to learn more about them. I suggest using a simple, multiple-choice survey, with just a few important questions that they can fill out quickly at the point of purchase.

However, you must compensate them for their time, either with a discount or a free offer on their next visit. This encourages them to come back a second time, which should be a critical part of your marketing formula, and thanks them for sharing this vital information.

Once you have the completed surveys, begin to graph the results to learn more about your customers and their perception of your business. Below is an example of a survey and the metrics that can be developed over a month of business:

VIP Questionnaire

Thank you for visiting us today. We would like to offer you a 25% discount on your next visit. Please fill out this brief, 4-question survey to receive this special VIP offer.

How did you find us?   (Results for the Month*)
(a) Direct Mail: _____   (26%)
(b) Radio: _____   (18%)
(c) Saw Location: _____   (41%)
(d) Referred by a Friend: _____   (5%)
(e) Other, please explain: _____   (10%)

Please provide your home and work zip codes:

Home: _____   (42% live within same zip code)
Work: _____   (58% work within same zip code)
(Top zip codes should be ranked to develop best areas for future advertising)

Please Specify your Gender:

Male: _____ (37%)

Female: _____ (63%)

Please Select Your Age Range:

Under 18:_____ (2%)

18 to 25: _____ (41%)

26 to 35: _____ (37%)

36 to 50: _____ (13%)

50 to 65: _____ (6%)

65+: _____ (1%)

Note: The numbers and text in parenthesis do not appear in the survey; they are just illustrating the data results gathered after a month of surveys.

If you would like to gather e-mail and home addresses, offer a VIP Club on the other side of the survey. Promise to provide them with additional savings, offers and incentives in exchange for providing this information.

As you create your survey, please be sure to keep it brief and focus on the data that is most important to your business. Consider why you are asking each question. Ideally, the information you gain will help you to determine your product offerings, your prices, your advertising mix, the geographic areas where you advertise, your coupons and special offers, and the development of your corporate image.

If you don't have a location, then mail your survey to your customer database, with a similar offer. As you can see, this form of data is critical to your marketing formula.

Geo-Mapping: The zip code question above is designed to determine where your customers are coming from. This is critical to your marketing planning. You may have an Internet business, so you would not think this data is important, but it is. Are your customers urban or rural, located in the Midwest, or on the East Coast? You must know this information so you can tailor your offers accordingly. For example, if you sell clothing on the Internet and you have few sales in the Northeast, you may want to offer a winter clothing line that appeals to this part of the country. You may also want to concentrate your advertising in those areas where you are most successful, or plan a brand launch in the areas that you are under-serving.

In many cases, you can track the geography of your customers without a formal survey. If they pay by check, credit card, or invoice you will have their addresses and can gather the same data. Only in a cash-oriented transaction will this question be needed on your survey.

Gathering Addresses & E-mail Addresses: When you meet your customers in person, you have the unique opportunity to request their addresses and e-mail information. The most important asset of your business will be your customer database. Once you have a complete customer database, you are able to "invite" your customers to do business with you again, by sending them special offers, coupons, and invitations. Focus these offers on the slow areas of your business, or to build traffic during the slower days in your location. Again, gathering e-mail addresses will allow you to keep in touch with your customers on a regular basis. You can send them links to your website, special offers, links to your corporate blog or Facebook page, and e-newsletters. All of these communications serve to build a closer relationship with your customer.

Many of us are uncomfortable providing this information. So it will be important to offer something special to the people who are willing to provide their addresses, like special discounts, special treatment (through VIP Clubs) or special products. Just think what it would take you to provide your address to a business, and apply that to your offer. Also, be sure to guarantee in writing that their data will be retained safely within your company, will be held in confidence and not shared with any other company or entity.

Product Introductions: When customers visit your location, you have a unique opportunity to introduce them to your new products and services. This can be done through up-selling and cross-selling, as well as introduced during their purchase. At the end of showing them the new product or service, ask them what they think, and record your findings. You can also ask them to "Tell a Friend", which will assist you in building your business.

Bounce-Back Coupons: Most consumers have well-defined shopping patterns, where they frequent the same businesses for the same products and services. This is true for every business category, whether it is a commercial printer, a restaurant, an auto mechanic, or a florist. It will often take a special offer, a new menu, the recommendation of a friend, or a compelling invitation for consumers to alter their established shopping patterns and try a new business. Once the consumer tries a new business, it is critical that he be given a reason to return again and again. These frequent visits will then establish this new business as part of their shopping pattern grid. A cost-effective way to bring new customers back to your business is by offering them a bounce-back coupon. The special offer associated with the bounce back coupon must be of value significant enough to compel the new customer to visit the business again. A free appetizer, oil change, 25% off their next purchase – whatever you believe will be effective in breaking through the established shopping pattern. Studies have shown that it will take approximately 7 visits to your business in order for it to become part of a consumer's shopping pattern.

It will be important to test different types of bounce-back coupon offers. You can track your bounce-back coupon response rates by collecting the redeemed coupons to see which offers are resonating with your new customers. Also, be sure to attach a copy of their sales receipt to each coupon so you can also track the resulting sales of each visit. This will allow you to determine the revenue generated by each bounce-back offer. You will quickly see that bounce-back coupons can be a very profitable enterprise. However, you will not see the impact on your business unless and until you set-up a procedure for tracking the metrics derived from your bounce-back coupon campaign. An example of results follows:

Example: March Campaign Results

Bounce-Back Campaign: # of Coupons Redeemed; Resulting Revenue
25% Off Next Visit: 88 coupons redeemed; $4,400 in resulting revenue
Free Appetizer: 43 coupons redeemed; $3,255 in resulting revenue
Free Margarita: 175 coupons redeemed; $3,500 in resulting revenue
Free Dessert: 23 coupons redeemed; $1,978 in resulting revenue
Buy 1 Get 1 Free – Entrée: 59 coupons redeemed; $2,950 in resulting revenue

Tracking your results will not only help you determine which of the bounce-back coupon offers are more effective for driving consumer traffic back to your business, it will also tell you which of the offers are best for driving revenue and profits. You can add columns to the tracking sheet that calculate your margins and net profits on the resulting revenue.

You can also consider embedding your bounce-back coupons into VIP Club Membership programs with consistent discounts and offers, coupon books with several coupons to choose from, or into your register receipts. Just be sure to state the value of the offer when you hand the coupon to your customer: **"This offer is an invitation for you to try our business again. You will receive a free margarita on your next visit. That is a savings of $8.00. Thank you again for visiting us."**

Without stating the value proposition of using the bounce-back coupon on their next visit, the consumer may not fully appreciate the offer and may discard it. However, if you tell them the value of the offer, in this case $8.00, the consumer is more likely to take advantage of it. Without the explanation, it is just a piece of paper, while with the explanation it has the value of an $8.00 bill. Few consumers will discard an $8 bill (if there were such a thing!).

Tracking Average Ticket per Customer: What is the average amount of money that each consumer spends on a single visit to your business? Calculate this number and begin to track it. Then develop up-selling, cross-selling, and special offer programs to increase your average ticket per customer. An example follows:

Example: Tracking Average Ticket Per Customer

Month / # of Customers / Total Sales / Average Ticket per Customer

January: 2,456 customers; $31,928 in Sales; a $13.00 Average Ticket per Customer
February: 2,315 customers; $32,410 in Sales; a $14.00 Average Ticket per Customer
March: 2,750 customers; $41,250 in Sales; a $15.00 Average Ticket per Customer
April: 2,693 customers; $45,781 in Sales; a $17.00 Average Ticket per Customer
May: 2,995 customers; $52,412 in Sales; a $17.50 Average Ticket per Customer

As you can see by the example above, the average ticket per customer for this business is increasing each month. It generally does not happen like this, but it exhibits the power of an increasing average ticket per customer. Getting new customers to visit your business location is often difficult, while encouraging your customers to spend more money once they visit your business is often easy. The key is implementing a program and tracking the results.

If your business averages 100 customers per day, and your average ticket per customer is $13.00, your daily sales will be $1,300 – or approximately $39,000 per month. However, if you are successful in increasing the average ticket per customer to $17.00, your daily sales will be $1,700 - or approximately $51,000 per month. This is a net increase of $12,000 per month. This would be the difference between profit and loss for many, many businesses. Moving this needle is not difficult. You just need a formula.

Relative to the other chapters in this book, this chapter on metrics has been long. There is a simple reason for this – metrics are critical to your business. You have now seen sufficient examples of tracking metrics in different ways. There are several important metrics to track. A list with a short explanation of each is below. Be sure to incorporate tracking mechanisms for each of the following:

Tracking Customer Demographics: Who are your customers?

Tracking Customer Addresses / Geography: Where do my customers come from?

Tracking Number of Visits for Each Customer: How often do my customers visit my business?

Tracking Value of Each Customer: How much do my customers spend with me each month / year? Knowing the value of each customer is very powerful when you are training your employees (and reminding yourself) of the value of providing terrific customer service.

Tracking Product Sales Relationships: What products sell best? Who buys each product? How often do my customers buy each product?

Tracking Number of Visits per Day / Event: How many customers visit my business each day? How many people visit my business during Happy Hour?

Tracking Customer Referrals: How many of my customers visit me by referral? (Then ask how you can increase these numbers.)

Contest & Drawing Results: How many people entered my contest? How much did they spend in my business during their visit in which they entered? How did this contest compare with my past contests?

Tracking Sales by Employee: Who is my top sales person? Who needs additional training?

Tracking Sales by Hour / Day / Week: When do my customers visit my business? What days and times are we the busiest? How does Saturday compare with other days of the week? What time of day do they visit my business? (This allows you to make critical staffing and hours of operation decisions.)

The combination of all of these tracking activities will change your business. The success of your business rests on having answers to a series of critical questions, and metrics can provide those answers. With your metrics in place, you will have the ability to make critical decisions about where to advertise, what offers and approaches work best, who your best employees are, what your hours of operation should be, how to staff your business, what products are selling, and (most importantly) who your customers are.

These are formula results. And they lead to critical formula decisions.

CHAPTER 4:
DEFINING YOUR TARGET CUSTOMER

Every business, no matter how large or small, is essentially a composition of customers. Without customers, you don't have a business. Customers define the business and serve as the lifeblood. Customers are the engine that drives the business. Customers influence the personality of a business. They should define the prices that a business charges and ultimately determine the product line. In short, customers are the most important part of any business.

The most important function of marketing is understanding who your customers are and developing strategies to reach them. Defining your target customer is the beginning of any marketing formula. Most marketing fails when this important step is by-passed or left for later. The reason for this is the customer is the natural outcome of your marketing formula or marketing plan.

Before you begin an experiment, it is highly advisable that you have a predictive outcome. Otherwise, you may be designing your experiment incorrectly. The outcome determines the processes, steps, and scope of the experiment. This is also true with developing a business, investing in it and operating it, without knowing who your target customer is. The reason this is so important is once you have defined your target customer, you have greatly simplified the scope of your marketing formula. You can rule out whole segments of the population and, therefore, many potential marketing channels. With a well-defined target customer, you can craft your marketing plan to precisely reach that customer. Let me give you a few examples.

Prestige Printing:

Prestige Printing provides printing and copies for high-end law firms. They offer excellent customer service, high quality reproduction, incredible reliability, and have developed security systems to ensure that everything they copy or print is kept absolutely confidential.

The printing and copying industry offers prices 40% lower than Prestige Printing, and yet this printing company is highly successful. They are located on the first floor of an impressive high-rise office building, surrounded by other impressive high-rise office buildings. These buildings are filled with prestigious law firms.

The staff at Prestige Printing dress like their customers. They are dressed professionally, wearing heels, jackets, ties, and business suits. The Prestige Printing office is spotless. Classical music can be heard while you wait. Customers can help themselves to a deluxe, complimentary coffee and tea bar. They have a comfortable waiting area, with well appointed furnishings and they offer free wireless Internet access and a comfortable working environment. Their hours of operation are from 5:00 am to 12:00 pm. They have a reputation for working quickly and precisely. They offer house accounts to their customers.

You are the owner of Prestige Printing. How do you begin your marketing plan?

Much of the marketing plan has already been written for you. That is because the customer has already been defined. And the Prestige Printing customer has defined the business. The location of the business was selected to best serve their high-end law firm customers. The hours of operation, decor, coffee bar, and employee dress have all been defined by the customer. The pricing structure, a full 40% higher than the marketplace, has also been defined by the customer.

The fact is, Prestige Printing is a direct reflection of its customers. It operates as an extension of its customer's businesses. Your business should as well.

So, as the owner of Prestige Printing, how do you begin your marketing plan? You begin by eliminating those areas that are not necessary. This is easy to do. You are only interested in high-end law firms. Wisdom in business is not so much figuring out what you need to do, but figuring out what you need *not* do. The following is a sample list of the marketing and advertising vehicles that you can rule out from the Prestige Printing marketing plan:

You **do not** need to:

- Market to Consumers
- Market to other cities or areas outside the downtown area
- Advertise on Radio, TV, Cable, Bus Benches, or Billboards
- Sponsor sports teams or advertise in church programs
- Hire an aggressive telemarketing firm
- Add bold, vibrant graphics to company vehicles
- Develop a wide-spread direct mail campaign

And the list goes on.

Rather, you can develop a marketing plan that carefully targets your ideal client. Here is an example of the marketing tactics and vehicles that you may elect to use for Prestige Printing.

Example: Prestige Printing Marketing Plan Elements

- Develop a professional sales staff with contacts within the law community
- Develop a database of the law offices that fit your customer profile within the downtown geographic area
- Within the database, include the contact information for the legal assistants that work within each of these firms. Include a list of their copy and printing equipment, so you know their in-house capabilities.
- Publish a professional newsletter that focuses on news about the local legal community. Mail these newsletters to your database and drop off copies for your contacts within each firm. Feature the products and services available at Prestige Printing within the newsletter.
- Join a local trade group for the legal industry. Advertise in this trade group's publication (or offer to print it for them) and be an active member of the group, providing speakers, social events, lunch meetings, etc....
- Develop a website that clearly defines your corporate mission to serve the legal community.
- Develop an SEO strategy that ranks you at the top of copies for the law industry in this downtown area.
- Develop a confidential ftp website for document storage for each of your clients.
- Print special delivery boxes, with your logo, for your printing and copy work that is designed to keep the contents safe and confidential while promoting your prestigious brand.
- Insert a small, professional brochure in every delivery box that thanks the customer for his business and provides a quick overview of your services.
- Develop tracking metrics for each of these activities so you can measure their effectiveness.

And the list goes on.

The marketing formula does not need to be complicated. However, it does need to be consistent with the identity of your target customers. It also needs to be consistently implemented and refined. Over time, this marketing formula will yield excellent results.

Let's contrast this marketing plan with a different type of business.

Kid's Fun Gym:

Kid's Fun Gym is filled with colorful soft mats, giant balls, and climbing structures. Silly, kid-oriented music plays all day. The staff is young and energetic (they have to be!) and they wear colorful sweat outfits. Kid's Fun Gym is located in a large shopping center, near a major grocery store, dry cleaners, and popular coffee shop. The shopping center is close to several elementary schools, surrounded by thousands of single family homes. Kid's Fun Gym offers mommy and toddler development classes, after-school gymnastics programs, exercise work outs for children, and is a popular destination for children's birthday parties on weekends. They have three vans painted brightly with the company colors, logo, and images of kids at play, loaded with equipment and activities for hosting on-site parties and events at local parks, beaches and homes. The staff has been carefully vetted, with a series of background checks; certificates for safety training and education line a small wall near the reception counter. Kid's Fun Gym offers a sophisticated security system that accounts for every child and a procedure for checking the children in and out of the facility with defined codes and approvals.

You are the owner of Kid's Fun Gym. How do you begin your marketing plan?

To save time and energy, could you just copy the marketing plan from Prestige Printing? Will this work? Of course not. Kid's Fun Gym has a completely different target customer. As a result, you will need to have a completely different marketing plan. You can rule out just about all of the marketing vehicles used by Prestige Printing. The elements of the marketing plan for Kid's Fun Gym may include the following:

Example: Kid's Fun Gym Marketing Plan Elements:

- Advertise on the shopping carts and register tape of the grocery store within your shopping center.
- Develop a cross-marketing program with the coffee shop and dry cleaners within your shopping center (they share many of the same customers).
- Sponsor programs and activities at the schools within your community.
- Develop a direct mail list for all of the homes with children within your community.
- Develop an active direct mail program to these homes.
- Develop a special Birthday Program for all of the children within your marketing radius. This special birthday party offer will be mailed to the child 6 weeks and 3 weeks prior to their birthday. Take them off your mailing list when they reach 10 years of age, unless they have younger siblings.
- Advertise in a local parents-oriented magazine.
- Develop a social networking strategy (Facebook, Twitter, LinkedIn, WordPress).
- Survey your customers. Learn who they are, what they like to do, where they shop, and what is important to them.
- Donate your services to the churches within your community for special events and pass-out flyers promoting your programs and location.

Kid's Fun Gym is a direct reflection of its customers. The customer has defined the business.

My earlier statement is worth repeating. The marketing formula does not need to be complicated. However, it does need to be consistent with the identity of your target customers. It also needs to be consistently implemented and refined. Over time, this marketing formula will yield excellent results. Just as our earlier example will for Prestige Printing.

These two small examples are not meant to emulate your business, or provide you with specific examples for developing your marketing plan. You may have a large business with thousands of employees, or a sophisticated Internet business that reaches the world. You will need entirely different elements within your marketing plan. However, the principles are the same.

Your business has customers. You need to focus your marketing in the places that your customers frequent. You need to understand their perspectives, appeal to their interests, and motivate them to do business with you. Timing is also important. American consumers need tax services in the late winter and early spring, they need retirement homes when they reach their late seventies and early eighties, and they need educational products when their children are under their roof. Psychology is an important part of marketing. It's all about understanding your customer.

There are many books that break down the different aspects of the paragraph above. They explore the pathos, ethos, and geo-focus of customer profiling. While these factors are incredibly important to your marketing formula, they are not the focus of this book. The goal of this book is to underscore the importance of developing a marketing formula for your business and then assist you in creating it. The specific details of that formula will likely come from other places, and other books.

With that said, there is a short list of things you need to know about your customer, before you develop your marketing formula.

What You Need To Know About Your Customer:

Who are they? Marketing folks use the term 'Demographics" when they refer to the simple question of "Who are they?" Don't let the big marketing terms intimidate you. They represent very simple concepts.

You need to know your customers' approximate age, their gender, their ethnicity, their education level, their income level, their level of net worth, and (sometimes) their religious affiliation.

Are they married? Single? Recently divorced? Do they have children? If so, how many children? How old are their children? Do they have parents? How old are their parents?

You need to know what they like to do for fun, the types of jobs they hold, how they spend their free time, and whether they use the Internet frequently. Do they like to travel? Are they into sports? Which sports? Are they into science? Are they into sports science? Do they drive big cars, small cars, or ride bicycles? Do they use public transportation? Are they healthy, or overweight? Do they work long hours, or are they retired? Do they own their own businesses, or do they work for someone else?

And, what is the best way to learn who they are?

Where are they? Marketing folks like to use the term "Geographics" to refer to the simple question of "Where are they?" This is another simple concept.

You need to know where your customers live. What is their zip code? Do they live in the city, the suburbs, or in the country? Do they rent apartments, or do they own single-family homes? Do they still live with their parents? What is the approximate value of the home they live in? How long have they lived in their current home? How long is their commute to work? How do they get to work? What route do they take to work?

Where do your customers work? Are they in professional office buildings, industrial warehouses, retail businesses, hospitals, or all of the above? Are they in specific industries? Are they bakers, lawyers, doctors, nurses, restaurant owners, engineers, school teachers, or marketing professionals? Do they work in the Midwest, on the West Coast, in the Pacific Northwest, on the East Coast, or in the South? Do they live and work in a foreign country? Do they travel long distances to work? Are they hopping commercial planes, or do they walk to work?

Where do they shop? How often do they shop? What do they buy? Do they shop on the Internet? What websites do they frequent? Are they loyal to the same businesses? Do they use Social Media? Do they have landlines or cell phones?

What do they care about? And how do they think? Marketers use the term "Psychographics" to refer to the psychological composition of consumers. It is another intimidating term to refer to "what do they care about?" or "how do they think?"

Again, the concept behind the term is simple. In this case, it could refer to what your customer's value. For example, do they place a higher value on saving money, or on saving time? Learning this key differentiator will shape your marketing formula. Do they like to use coupons, or would they prefer VIP membership cards? Are coupons offensive to them?

How were they raised? Are they hyper-consumers, conscientious about the latest fashions, or are they frugal and more focused on building their net worth?

Are they socially and environmentally aware? Do they value the environment and are they eager to recycle? Do they volunteer their time and tithe to their church? Are they liberal, conservative, or moderate? Are they into what is hip and cool, or are they more focused on the welfare of their family (not to say these two perspectives are at odds with one another!)? Do they value freedom? Are they patriotic? What are they most afraid of? Is security a concern? Do they enjoy their privacy, or are they active in society? What kinds of music do they like? Do they prefer going to the symphony or to a rock concert? Do they prefer the museum or the mall? Are they likely to share their experiences with their friends, or do they want to keep their ideas to themselves?

What are they thinking now? What will they do next? Are they into big houses and big cars, or are they moving into smaller houses and smaller electric cars? Are they wealthy or poor, or somewhere in between? Are they thinking about helping their parents find and fund a first class retirement home, or are they trying to save for their kid's college fund – or both. Do they have debt? How much? Do they need financial help, or are they able to offer help to others?

Do they think Elvis is cool, or do they prefer Hanna Montana?

Psychographics are more difficult to pin down. It is possible to make marketing assumptions based on the combination of demographics, geographics and prevailing social trends. For example, if you know your customers are between the ages of 18 and 25, they live on the West Coast, they are middle-income and they snowboard frequently, there is a high probability that they are currently Internet savvy, own an iPad, and care about the environment.

But how do you know for sure? In fact, how do you know any of these things about who your customers are, where they live, or what they think? It's simple....... you ask them!

How do you ask them? With surveys, focus groups, and intercept questions.

Surveys: You are probably very familiar with surveys. You have probably answered a few of them over the years. Typically, you receive a discount or a special offer to answer a few, simple questions. The longer and more personal the surveys, usually the better the resulting gift or discount. There are college courses based on marketing research and developing an accurate survey. Many books are focused on this subject, but this is not one of them. I will just give you a few simple things to consider, as you develop your survey:

- **Keep them short.** Make sure the respondent can complete the survey quickly. They may resent the time it takes to complete a long survey and you don't want them to resent the experience and not continue shopping with you. They also may not complete the survey. Before you begin, ask your team what are the 2-3 things you really need to know about your customers? Just ask a few questions on each survey.
- **Keep them simple.** Avoid long and confusing sentences and potentially unfamiliar terms. Don't assume your customers have specific knowledge of something within your industry. Keep the concepts universal. Try to keep your questions down to 3 to 7 words.
- **Prioritize.** Ask your most important questions first to make sure they you receive the answers you need. Eliminate the lower priority questions and just keep the top few.
- **Warm them up.** Don't ask the more personal questions first (like annual income or marriage status). Begin with the less objectionable questions, like "Home Zip Code?" Also, ask the easiest questions first, and the more detailed comment –oriented questions last.

- **How will you measure the responses?** Multiple choice questions allow you to develop meaningful metrics, while open-ended comments give you insight into potential changes within your business. Both are valuable. But what are your objectives? If you are trying to decide what percentage of your clients are female, then a simple two choice question will yield simple results. However, if you would like your customers to help you improve your product line selection, you may need to use more open-ended questions.

Focus Group: Do you want your customers to tell you what they really think? Is a simple survey not enough? Then developing a focus group is a great way to lean more about your customers.

Typically, focus groups are conducted by a third party company, advertising agency, or a neutral moderator. They are often taped, or watched by the client from behind one-way glass. The participants are usually paid for their time, approximately $100 for an hour-long focus group. There are usually 5 to 12 participants that fit the core target demographic. Within this setting, the moderator can ask the group a series of questions, share a new product, review a new television commercial or print advertisement, or just ask questions about the business in question. Within a series of carefully planned focus groups, you can learn a great deal about who your customers are and what they think.

The results of focus groups can be powerful. Corporate strategies have been rewritten, products cancelled and advertising plans scrapped due to negative reviews. The key to the focus group is setting aside your personal passions and bias and *listening* to what your customers think. This is not as easy as it sounds. If you listen carefully and check your ego at the door, you can learn a lot from a series of focus groups and potentially make your company, or save your company, a fortune.

Intercepts: Intercepts, often called mall intercepts because that is where they often take place, act like a small, less controlled focus group. Third party companies, company employees or the CEO can facilitate a mall intercept. In practice, the mall intercept is simply walking up to an individual within a shopping mall that appears to fit your core demographic and asking them a few questions. The participants are generally not paid for their time, but some level of discount or compensation can be a good idea.

Let's say you have a new company logo in the works and you are down to the top three selections. Within the context of a mall intercept, you would walk up to your core demographic, let's say women that appear to be between the ages of 35 and 54 (these ages will have to be approximated, as it will not be safe to ask strange women in a mall how old they are!). Simply walk up to them and say, "Excuse me, my company is trying to decide which of these three logos we should choose, can you please help us?" You will be surprised at how easy it is to conduct a mall intercept and how much information you will glean from it.

Before you head off to the mall with samples of your glossy new direct mail campaign, be sure to set some objectives. How many intercepts do you need? How will you avoid influencing the participant's decisions? What will you ask them? Will you reveal the identity of your company? What times and days will be best to find high numbers of your apparent core demographic? How will you record and calculate your results? How many malls will you go to (you may have a different response in a suburban mall, when compared to a mall within the city). And so on. It is always best to have a plan (a formula) for your marketing activities, especially when you are interacting directly with your target client.

Data Analytics / Customer Profiles: Technology is used widely in marketing to define the profile of a customer. If you have a database of your current customers, with their name and address, there are analytic programs that will tell you who these customers are.

Let's say you have a database of the people who have done business with you over the last 12 months; you can send this database to one of several data analytics companies and, for a fee, they are able to profile your customer list. The profile report will tell you where your customers live (urban / suburban / rural), how old they are, their education level, their net worth level, their income level, their religious affiliation, their marital status, number of children, and the ages of those children. Some of these profile reports can tell you what these people like to do for fun, their affiliations and values. All of this data is extremely powerful in the hands of an experienced marketer.

Why do you want to know who your current customers are? Two main reasons: (1) to make sure that you continue to connect with them so they will remain your customers, and (2) to find more customers just like the ones you currently have.

Once you have a profile of your customers, you can provide this profile to a direct mail, marketing, or list broker company and acquire a database of people or businesses that match this profile. If your core customer is male, 35 to 54, well-educated, lives in the suburbs, married with children, has owned a home for over 5 years and lives within a 10 zip code area, then you can purchase a list equal to the size of your customer database and develop a campaign to reach these new target customers.

Your business has corporate clients, rather than individual consumers? No problem! You can also profile your corporate clients. You may find that your business client profile consists of companies that have between 10 and 25 employees, sales of over $3 million, located within 7 zip codes, and focused within 15 different SIC codes (business types). You can then use this client profile to purchase a new list of target companies that fit your corporate profile. You can effectively double the size of your client base by using a profile technique. These programs come in all sizes and price points, so be sure to shop around. I have seen reports offered in the $400 range all the way up to $50,000. In most cases, these programs are worth their weight in gold, as they can quickly accelerate your company's growth. So long as you have a formula developed for reaching these new prospective clients and converting them into customers.

Additionally, it is important to develop a formula to retain your existing customers. Invite them to visit your company again. Provide them with incentives to try new products and services, ask them for referrals to their friends. Customer retention strategies will be covered in more detail in Chapter 14.

The cornerstone of your formula marketing must be your customer. You must understand exactly who your customer is *before* you develop your marketing formula. Develop the profile, put it down in writing, attach photos of who these people or businesses are, post it on a bulletin board, and begin to peel the layers of your core customer. What do they think about? What do they care about? Where do they live? Where do they shop? How do they get to work? Where do they work? Why would they decide to do business with you?

If you can unlock the mysteries of your core customer, then you can build a very powerful marketing formula.

CHAPTER 5:
DIFFERENTIATE YOUR COMPANY

Let's go back to the last question we asked in the previous chapter. Why would these potential customers want do business with you? As you know, the consumer has many, many choices. You probably have many competitors. You may also compete with unrelated industries.

For example, if you own a restaurant, you are competing with every other restaurant for the customer's entertainment dollar. Additionally, you are competing with the movie theatre, the zoo, the ice rink, the symphony, Netflix, the Internet, the beach, and other entities competing for the consumer's entertainment time and dollar.

Today's consumers have more choices than they have ever had before. And they now have sophisticated search engines that provide them with more information about their options, what other people think of them, and how much money they should cost. As a marketer, your job of attracting new customers has never been more difficult. Therefore, you must differentiate your company from all of the rest – from all of your competitors and the other options available to your customer.

How do you do this?

Identifying your market differentiator is not an overnight process. It takes some time, thought, and brainstorming. You are essentially looking for the key value propositions that will compel the consumer to select your business over other businesses. A good way to sort out the possibilities is to develop a Situational Analysis, within the process of writing your marketing plan. In the next chapter, we will be developing the classic 5-Step Marketing Plan as the basis for your marketing formula. However, before we dive into the heart of this fascinating process (and I mean this sincerely), let's discuss the core of differentiation.

You Have Three Options – But You Can Only Select Two

There is an old maxim in marketing that states that the consumer can select two out of three options from the following list:

- Best Quality
- Best Service
- Best Price

So they can select Best Quality and Best Service, but they cannot have Best Price at the same time – or quality and service will need to be sacrificed.

If they select Best Price, they can still have Best Service, but they cannot possibly have Best Quality and so on.

Some refer to this as the Business Triangle. According to the laws of physics and business, you can only have two of these three choices. But I don't think this is true any more. Or at least it is not that black and white.

With the advent of automation, technology, the Internet, and burgeoning and accessible low-cost labor markets (like China, India, Cambodia and others) it is now possible for the consumer to select all three – or at least that is what many companies are promising. Search the Internet, visit the mall, talk with friends and you will quickly see that there are companies out there that are offering all three: Best Quality, Best Service, and Best Price.

The Internet has changed everything. You can now buy your Mercedes (Best Quality) on the Internet (Best Price) or from Costco (Best Price) rather than from your local auto dealer. You could make the claim that the Dealer provides the Best Service model that is missing from the Internet scenario, but that is not true. You can source your Mercedes on the Internet, buy the exact color and specifications that you are looking for (something you cannot easily do at a dealership) and have it delivered to your home (Best Service). This is one example.

I know there are marketers and business people that will read this and disagree with me. We can argue the point all day long. Meanwhile, consumers have been conditioned by the new reality, or the perception of it. The new marketplace has convinced them that they can have all three choices. If you would like them to be your customers, you need to let go of this old way of thinking and find a way to provide all three of the consumers' choices *simultaneously*. If you don't, someone else will. If you don't believe me, search for a hotel room at the Ritz. First call their reservation desk and get their standard price, then visit their website and search for their "Internet price", then do an Internet search for "Best Prices Rates at the Ritz" or something like it. You will suddenly find that you can have all three choices – or at least the perception of them, which is often good enough for the consumer.

As you craft your differentiation strategy, don't fall into the trap of thinking that there are limits to what you can offer. There may be obstacles to what is practical to offer, but there are also ways to remove these obstacles.

Key Points of Differentiation:

Let's ask ourselves again – Why does the consumer want to do business with you? What makes your company special? What can you do that the other guys aren't doing? A list follows, which may be worth considering. This is not a formal list of marketing differentiators. Rather, it is the foundational reason why a consumer might choose you over the other guys. It is important to strip away all of the marketing terms and focus on what is motivating the customer. Here we go:

- You are the easiest to do business with
- You are the most reliable to do business with
- You have the best reputation in the marketplace
- You know them better
- They know you better
- You are invested in their success
- They can get everything they need in one place
- Their friends do business with you
- You are fun to do business with
- It is cool to do business with you
- It is exciting to do business with you
- You have many new things to offer
- You have the best prices
- They don't have to worry
- They like you
- You are very close to their home / office
- It is easy to park
- You have drive-through – so they don't have to get out of their car
  (my wife selected our bank on this basis)
- You care about them
- You will save them time
- You will make them look like a super hero
- Their family, friends, neighbors, and co-workers will think they are cool / smart / savvy
- They will receive peace of mind
- You listen to them
- You have the best selection
- You have the most knowledgeable people
- You care about them

This is not an elegantly written list, with sleek marketing terms for a reason. You need to get down to the basics with your customers. You need to figure out what they want most. You learned who they are in the last chapter and now you need to deliver what they want.

This should be a messy process. I'm talking flip charts, plenty of coffee, colored pens, sales data, customer profiles, survey results, and a lot of shouting. Map it out. What makes you different? Why do your customers do business with you? Why should other people want to do business with you? What are you better at than anyone else in the world? How can you communicate it? How can you guarantee it? How can you offer it to everyone?

Are you a retail business? Got nothing special to offer? What if you are 10 minutes closer than any other business in your market space? Target the people that would agree with this value proposition and market this message consistently. Then find and promote other ways that you can save them time – free home delivery, special parking spaces, advance reservations, easy to use check-out, best selection, other items they need in the same place, etc…

Are you a contractor who builds large residential homes? Then focus on your reputation. Gather positive testimonials and share them with your clients. Develop professional photographs of the work you have done. Convey a high-quality image. Prove to your target customers that you are easy to work with, that you will do a good job, that you will show up and deliver their project on time and within budget. Develop procedures that make sure this always happens. Then communicate these to your customers.

It's time to brainstorm. Ask these questions over and over. Over time the pillars that hold your business up over all the rest will begin to appear. You will separate yourself from the pack and you will have a different story, a compelling reason, or a killer application that will cause consumers to select you over other companies.

Surf Brothers Teriyaki:

We will conclude this chapter with an example of a company that has a very simple and effective differentiation strategy. In fact, their business formula is so simple that it seems to lack stability, yet the business is an overwhelming success. I will let them tell you the story of their business in their own words, the same words they use on their website:

Graduating high school, Reza, at the age of 18, had a dream of opening up a restaurant that would serve the best teriyaki chicken and beef in San Diego. After borrowing a small amount of money from friends and family, Reza and his father opened up a hole-in-the-wall restaurant called Tokyo's Teriyaki in November of 1992. Struggling with no funds to advertise and being completely unknown in Encinitas, (a coastal community in San Diego) we became a local hot-spot only through word of mouth. Word spread because Reza and his father would pay attention to every single customer, making sure every plate served was the most delicious teriyaki plate customers would ever have.

As their reputation grew outside of Encinitas, customers from other cities asked them to open up in their neighborhood. Looking to expand, Reza's younger brother, Amir, joined the family business after graduating from La Costa Canyon High School in 1997 and opened up their second location in San Marcos and changed their name to Island Brothers Teriyaki.

With a new name, Surf Brothers Teriyaki, and seven locations, Reza and his family have not forgotten their original roots, passion and loyalty to their customers.

This is a good story. A story that resonates with the Surf Brothers' core demographics, namely health conscious consumers looking for a fast-food alternative, middle income to upper middle income, primarily in their 20s and 30s, who place a value on their time. It is very important to note that the menu at Surf Brothers is very different from other restaurants. For the first 17 years of business, there were only three items on the menu:

- Chicken ($7.29)
- Steak ($7.79)
- Combo: Chicken & Steak ($7.59)

They recently added two additional items:
- Shredded Chicken Sliders Plate ($3.79)
- Lite Bite ($4.99)

You can also order sides of rice, salad, and chicken or steak skewers. The menu is so streamlined that ordering your meal at Surf Brothers is an uncomplicated joy.

"The simple menu was intentional," explains Amir Karkouti, the youngest of the Surf Brothers. "We wanted to create a process that would control quality and maintain efficiency, like Henry Ford's conveyor belt production system for the early automobile."

At lunch, you will always find a line at Surf Brothers Teriyaki, but the simple menu keeps the line moving very quickly. Customers are served in less than a minute (I have personally field-tested this claim several times and have confirmed its validity). This serves their core demographic well. They are hungry, on a budget, and in a hurry, but they want to eat healthy. Surf Brothers has developed a simple formula for serving up just what their customers want.

"We knew we could serve our meals quickly," Amir remembers. "But we were inconsistent. Sometimes it would take 5 or 10 minutes. We saw that we had an opportunity to offer a unique dining experience if we could just serve all of the meals in under a minute."

The brothers sat down for a business brainstorming session and asked how they could design a process that would serve their customers in under a minute. It was a bold claim, and bold ideas carried it through. Within two weeks, Surf Brothers had implemented a hub-and-spoke system that allowed them to prepare their food from a central kitchen, while making just-in-time deliveries to their restaurants. This gave the Surf Brothers the efficiency of serving their meals in under a minute, while maintaining the slow cooked quality and taste of cooking their meats for over 40 minutes.

"Our restaurants are located in business parks and industrial areas," said Amir. "Our customers have about 30 minutes to eat lunch. We wanted them to be able to eat high-quality food and feel good when they go back to their offices."

All of the items on their menu are priced competitively, especially for the size portion the consumer receives.

"Our portions are very unique," Amir continues. "It is very hard to find a restaurant, especially in the fast-food space, that offers a 10 oz. cut of chicken or 8 oz of steak. We weren't really focused on price. We wanted to give our customers a good value, healthy food in generous portions. Our meals are prepared like a home-cooked meal, without preservatives, microwaves, or rice cookers. We believe this is very important."

The Surf Brothers go on to explain their value proposition and differentiation strategy to their customers in a letter on their website and on the menus within their locations.

Dear Loyal Patrons,

We wanted to write to all of our loyal customers to explain in great detail the difference between us and other quick service establishments.

We receive a daily delivery of chicken. Our chicken is never frozen and needs to be prepared each and every day. This means no preservatives, MSG, or any other chemicals to keep the chicken fresh.

The chicken plate consists of 10 oz. of chicken and the steak plate has 8 oz. of steak. Those portions are hard to find at quick serve restaurants.

Both our chicken and our steak are minimally processed and contain no artificial ingredients.

Our meats are naturally lean, but our preps go a step further and trim most of the fat off our meats, for a healthier product. Our food is featured on Healthdiningfinder.com which lets consumers know that we strive to have healthy food choices for our customers.

Although customers receive their items in less than a minute, our plates take 25 to 40 minutes to cook, without microwaves, rice cookers that keep rice sitting all day, or other "quick" methods.

So the next time you eat at any of our Surf Brother Teriyaki locations, rest assured you are receiving dine-in quality food at "take-out" prices.

Sincerely,
Amir and Reza
The Surf Brothers

And there it is. They state their simple formula for setting their business apart from their competition. It is communicated simply and boldly: dine-in quality food at "take-out" prices. Well said, Surf Brothers! Every business needs to communicate their value proposition in a few, simple words. That's the key to an effective differentiation strategy.

The Surf Brothers offer their customers other unique value propositions not found together in other restaurants. Some of the claims are stated publicly, others are merely understood:

- Service in less than a minute
- Generous portions
- High-quality, healthy food
- A simple, no-frills menu
- A cool vibe that appeals to their core demographic
- A local appeal that connects with San Diego natives and recent transplants

"We are also careful to give back to the community," Amir said, providing the last of their value propositions. "We make donations to the local schools and play an active role. We value our customers and we want them to know that we care about them and their community."

When discussing how they communicate their unique value propositions, Amir was passionate about the importance of explaining them to his customers. "You can't expect your customers to know about your business. You have to teach them or show them."

Amir makes an excellent point. When you work every day in a business, you know your business well and you assume that your customer does, too. Amir uses YouTube video, direct mail, point-of-purchase, menus and their website to convey their value propositions consistently. The hard work is paying off. Surf Brothers Teriyaki has connected with its customers in a special way, converting them into a loyal sales force that return to its restaurants several times each month.

Surf Brothers Teriyaki provides a delicious example of how a business can differentiate itself from the competition. Once a company has created its differentiation strategy and defined its target customer, it becomes much easier to write the marketing plan. In fact, the marketing plan becomes an extension of the personality of the business.

In the next chapter, we will discuss the details of writing a marketing plan. Relax! It's easier than you think. Five easy steps and you are on your way – no matter how large or small your enterprise.

CHAPTER 6:
WRITING YOUR MARKETING PLAN

A marketing plan is like a map.

Imagine visiting a city for the first time. You hop into your rental car and leave the airport on your way to a specific destination, let's say the city's museum. You are in a hurry, so you decide not to ask for directions or to buy a map. You find the freeway on-ramp without much difficulty and you drive in the direction of where you think the city museum could be. Finally, after traveling up and down the freeway, testing different exits, looking for the downtown area, and taking many wrong turns, you find the museum.

Congratulations! You are proud of yourself. You did it without asking for directions and without a map. Amazing! Unfortunately, it took you three and a half hours, you are out of gas, and the museum is closed.

With a map and some directions, you could have arrived at the museum in 20 minutes. But you were in a hurry. You were too busy to stop and ask for help. You were too busy to plan your route. And now you have found your primary destination – but the museum is closed.

Many companies are on a journey like this one. They are in a hurry to get to their destination. They don't have time to stop for directions or buy a map. And they are driving up and down the business highways, searching for the right direction. They are operating without a marketing plan.

Sure, they will eventually find their way. By the process of elimination, they will eventually hire the right people, develop the right messaging strategy, make their sales goals, enter new markets, offer new products and services, and, perhaps, become profitable. However, if they had a map, they would have completed their journey in less time, for less money, and with fewer mistakes.

A good marketing plan is like a map. It gives you the directions you need to get to your destination quickly. It minimizes the wrong turns and conserves your resources. A marketing plan is one of the most important documents in your company. It should be the foundation of all of your marketing activities. Many companies work without a marketing plan, making their decisions as they go.

I have personally witnessed many companies that operate without a marketing plan and I can tell you that they waste a lot of money and time. They also have a difficult time defining their customer profile and communicating their value proposition. They often struggle to make a profit, and they don't understand why. Some may be successful, in spite of making it up as they go, but they would be so much more successful if they just had a marketing plan.

It is critical to begin with a marketing plan. Before you begin to implement your sales strategies, before you set your prices, before you make any advertising decisions, before you design your company website, *please* begin with a marketing plan.

How To Write Your Marketing Plan: The Classic 5-Step Plan

Writing a marketing plan does not need to be complicated. It should only take a few hours, not several weeks. It should focus on the areas that are most important to your business. It will also be a living document. It will change often.

I am not a fan of multi-page spiral-bound marketing plans that are written by professional agencies. They too often sit on a book shelf collecting dust.

A marketing plan should be just a few pages long. It should travel with you in your portfolio for easy reference and quick adjustments. It should be reviewed often to confirm that you are headed in the right direction. It should be consulted before you make a decision or turn your company in a certain direction.

For these reasons, I use a classic 5-step marketing plan.

The classic 5-step marketing plan has been used by large and small companies over several decades. It is simple, but comprehensive. It acts as the foundation of your marketing formula, while allowing you the flexibility to make changes. This 5-step plan is the format I have used to write marketing plans for the past 25 years. It is a simple, elegant formula that contains all of the elements of your marketing plan, while yielding results and the metrics necessary to evaluate the success of the strategies and tactics.

This is what it looks like:

5-Step Marketing Plan:
1. **Situational Analysis**
2. **Objectives**
3. **Strategies**
4. **Tactics**
5. **Assessment**

We will cover each of the steps and then get to work on writing your marketing plan. Your marketing plan will form the basis of your Formula Marketing.

Step 1 - Situational Analysis: What's Going On?

A Situational Analysis means exactly what you think – you analyze the situation surrounding your business. It is the first step in the classic 5-step marketing plans used by most major corporations, and many small companies, too.

In the last chapter, we discussed the importance of differentiation. In the chapter before it, we discussed the importance of defining your customer. Prior to that chapter, we discussed the importance of creating and studying your marketing metrics. The marketing plan will pull these important elements, and many others, together.

It is best to do your brainstorming work within the context of your marketing plan. As you decide what makes you different from the other guys, define your target customer, and pinpoint your key metrics, you can be doing these things within the framework of your marketing plan.

The Situational Analysis will contain these items. It is the funnel that you put everything into to develop the other steps of your marketing plan. Don't be intimidated by the title, a Situational Analysis is just a snapshot of your company in the marketplace.

Your Situational Analysis should include a brief summary of the factors surrounding your company. It should discuss those forces that are contributing to your company's success, or holding it back from attaining cash flow and profitability.

Here is an example of what your Situational Analysis should include:

I. Situational Analysis
- Your Industry
- Your Product Line
- Your Services
- Current Market Conditions
- Your Competition
- Your Capabilities
- Your Positioning within the Market
- Your Image
- In what areas are you better than your competition?
- In what areas are your competitors better than you?
- Current Sales
- Current Personnel
- Your Location
- Your Current Customer Profile
- Your Target Customers
- Your Current Resources
- Current Opportunities for Your Company
- Current Cash / Debt Position

- Current Cash-Flow Needs, Expenses
- Etc…

Try to summarize each of these important points in a few lines. Keep your Situational Analysis focused on the most critical and relevant details of each item. Try to keep your Situational Analysis to a few, brief paragraphs. If it is short and precise, you will read it often. If it is several long-winded pages, you will never read it again. Also, and most importantly, the act of keeping your Situational Analysis short will force you to focus on the most important, most critical aspects of your business.

Address each of these items as if it is a question:

What industry is your business in?

What products and services does your business offer?

Who are your customers?

And so on… This will simplify the process.

I recommend writing your Situational Analysis in a group setting. This helps you cover all of your bases, while building consensus within your organization.

A sample marketing plan will follow that illustrates what your Situational Analysis could include, as well as all of the other elements of the 5-step marketing plan. For now, we will cover each of the 5 steps in order.

Step 2 - Objectives: What are Your Goals?

Objectives are simply goals for your business. What do you hope to accomplish? What sales do you hope to achieve? What position do you hope to have within your marketplace?

It is important to set objectives that you can track and measure, so you know when you reach them. I often see corporate marketing plans that have offer no components that can be tracked. How then do you know if you accomplished your goals? Earlier in this book, I stated that the marketing department must be held accountable for its results. The key is developing clear objectives that can be tracked, measured, and analyzed. Here are some examples:

II. Objectives

- Increase Annual Sales by $2,000,000 over Previous Year
  (for Total Annual Sales of $18,000,000)
- Recruit 50 New Clients (at $20K average sales this year) = $1,000,000
- Open Region Two and Acquire 25 New Clients in This Region
- Retain All Current Clients (Total: 405) from Previous Year
- Increase Sales to Current Clients by $1,000,000 over Previous Year
- Become the Market Leader (requires total of 15% Market Share)
- Increase Sales for Product X by 20%

- Increase Average Transaction Amount from $2,800 to $3,000
- Launch New Service Y by end of Third Quarter
- Implement New Automated System for Operations Dept. by Year End
- Hire Four New Sales Representatives by Fourth Quarter
- Expand Database of Target Customers from 250 to 500 by Year End

As you can see, these objectives are very clear. They will either be accomplished, or they will not be. The results will speak for themselves. There will be no opportunity to hide behind vague conclusions.

On the other hand, objectives that make statements like: "become a better company", "open new markets", "become the best in the industry" lack the specifics to confirm whether or not they have been reached. Good objectives have numbers that are easy to calculate, percentages that can be verified, and specific deadlines. Good objectives offer no place to hide.

The objectives should also move your company forward. The results should help you increase your sales, launch new products, reach new customers, expand your company, and improve your position in the industry.

Finally, objectives should be attainable. Setting very high, unrealistic goals will let everyone off the hook. "Well, we knew increasing sales by 25% was impossible…at least we boosted sales by 3%" is a natural conclusion to many marketing plans. There is nothing wrong with a 3% increase (for a mature company), but this type of approach to your objectives will allow key executives to hide. You simply cannot allow that to happen.

Set objectives that are attainable, but also stretch your company to the next level. There is an old saying in business, "You are either growing, or you are going." It means that if you are not growing your sales, growing your market share, or growing your staff, that your competition is taking over a larger percentage of the available market. In other words, they are eating your lunch. They are absorbing your growth and taking your customers away from you. However, if you are growing your business, you are commanding a greater percentage of the market.

Setting objectives is exciting and best done in a group setting. It promotes new ideas, corporate "buy-in" and accountability to the results. It also allows the key players within your company to consider what is possible and contribute to the success of the company. It allows everyone to work together to build a road to a higher vantage point. To dream.

It is amazing what happens when you set big objectives for your company. Everyone gets excited. They all begin to contribute ideas for how to accomplish the objectives. It is a wonderful process for building "team" within a company.

Reaching your objectives will take hard work, on-time implementation, good execution, and maybe a little luck. Reaching a set of objectives doesn't just happen. Steps must be taken to make sure that they happen. You must have strategies in place to accomplish your objectives. And you must have tactics in place that accomplish your strategies. These, of course, are the next two steps of the marketing plan.

Step 3 - Strategies: How Are You Going to Get There?

Once you set your objectives, stand back and look at them. Then ask yourself, or your team, how are you going to get there? The "How" will comprise the core of your strategy.

For example, if your goal is to increase your average transaction amount from $250 to $350, you then need to ask yourself, "*How* can we add an average of $100 to every sale?" There are many answers to this question.

Your business type will be a key factor in how you answer the question. If you are a retail company, with sales staff and check-out counters, you may need to adopt an aggressive up-selling and cross-selling strategy, offer more products, increase the quantity of impulse items around the counter area, and do more suggestive selling from the floor.

If you are a custom manufacturer, you may need to sell certain add-ons or features, like warranties, special coatings, rush charges, packaging options, or additional related products.

If you provide professional services to your clients, you will need to add to your suite of services, enhance your current services, and/or suggest to your clients that they try some of the other services you offer.

In all of these scenarios, you may need to increase your prices for the products and services that your customers already purchase. However, before you just raise your prices, be sure that you have a value proposition in place that warrants the price increase. Today's consumers are very savvy, and they know when they are paying too much.

Some examples of marketing strategies follow:

III. Strategies

- Acquire New Clients for Region Two by Increasing Direct Sales Presence and Implementing Marketing Programs
- Increase Average Client Spend through Expanded Product Line and Up-Selling Programs
- "Lock In" Major Clients with Dependent Technologies and Services and enhanced Client Retention Programs
- Increase Average Sales by Sales Representatives with Improved Training and Marketing Support
- Become an Industry Leader by heightening Brand Name Recognition in the Marketplace
- Expand Market Share by Targeting the Key Clients of our Competitors
- Improve a Customer's Experience with our Company by implementing Improved Processes, Customer Service, and Follow-up Programs

These are good strategies. You can use versions of these for your company, or expand beyond them. Writing your strategies takes thought, but it always produces clarity for your company's mission. Once you have your strategies written, you need to step back from the whiteboard and ask "*How* will we accomplish these strategies?" Each will be accomplished by breaking them down into little steps that can be placed on your calendar and plugged into your budget. These little steps are called Tactics.

Step 4 - Tactics: The Things You Will Do

How will you accomplish your strategies? The answer is tactics.

Tactics are the series of things that you will do to accomplish your strategies. Tactics are the heart and soul of a marketing plan. In fact, most companies simply have a set of tactics, rather than an actual marketing plan.

Many marketing professionals make the mistake of just diving right into developing their marketing calendar, without taking the important steps of setting their strategy and identifying their objectives. Tactics are fun, often exciting, and represent the core of a marketing department's role. However, it is a big mistake to jump straight to tactics.

Before you cut the PO for the radio commercials, order your direct mail list, or design your new website, you must be sure that your tactics are aligned with your strategies and objectives. If they are not aligned, then you are wasting time and money.

The *how* of executing your strategy is accomplished through tactics. In our example, one of the strategies was "Acquire New Clients for Region Two by Increasing Direct Sales Presence and Implementing Marketing Programs". That sounds like a good strategy. Each strategy should be linked directly back to one, or several, of the stated objectives, like one that I listed earlier "Open Region Two and Acquire 25 New Clients in This Region".

A marketing plan is like a spider web, with all of the components - from the objectives to the strategies to the tactics - connected and woven tightly together. Or, for you classical music lovers, it should be composed like a symphony, with all sections of the orchestra working together in unison.

To accomplish each strategy, you will need to develop and implement the correct tactics. Some of these tactics may cross department lines and involve other parts of the business, like sales, operations and customer service. This is both expected and important. Remember that tactics are the tangible items or events that you will put into your marketing calendar and itemize within your marketing budget.

This is what they could look like for this strategy:

Strategy I: Acquire New Clients for Region Two by Increasing Direct Sales Presence and Implementing Marketing Programs

Tactic One: Hire Two New Sales Representatives in Region Two
Budget: $135,000 **Completion Date:** February 1st

Tactic Two: Hire One Customer Service Representative for Region Two
Budget: $53,000 **Completion Date:** January 15th

Tactic Three: Acquire Database for Region Two that Matches Current Customer Profile
Budget: $350 **Completion Date:** January 5th

Tactic Four: Design and Implement 12-Part Direct Mail Campaign with Landing Pages and E-Blast Opt-In that Includes Testimonial and Special Trial Offer
Budget: $25,000 **Completion Date:** January 11th

Tactic Five: Develop YouTube Video to Communicate Company Story and Differentiation to Region Two Target Customers
Budget: $2,500 **Completion Date:** January 11th

Tactic Six: Develop & Print "Region Two" Version of Current Marketing Collateral
Budget: $7,500 **Completion Date:** January 5th

Tactic Seven: Revise Website to Include Region Two
Budget: $1,500 **Completion Date:** January 5th

Tactic Eight: Develop Series of Press Releases for Region Two Trade Publications to Announce Launch, Tell Company Story, and Cover Expansion (with Press Kits)
Budget: $1,250 **Completion Date:** February 15 – October 31

Tactic Nine: Reserve Booth Location in the 3 "Region Two" Trade Shows; Reserve Trade Show Display for each event; Schedule Event Staff; Purchase Pens, Candy & Coffee Mugs; Print Trade Show Invitations and Follow-up Pieces; Post Trade Show Schedule on Website; Purchase Advertising in Trade Show Publications
Budget: $48,000 **Completion Date:** March 20th

Tactic Ten: Develop Testimonials from Current Region One Customers. Add testimonials to Marketing Collateral, Direct Mail Campaign, YouTube, Trade Show Advertisements, Website, Press Releases and provide to New Sales Staff
Budget: $0 **Completion Date:** November 1 (prior year)

Now you can see why the marketing department is always busy! There is a lot of work to be done to launch Region Two. Remember, the tactics above only cover one of the strategies. A different series of tactics will be needed to execute the other strategies listed earlier. Many of the tactics linked to other strategies will overlap and work together synergistically. A total of 30 to 50 tactics may be needed to execute each of the strategies and reach all of the stated objectives.

It is important to select tactics that will work. If you are not sure what works best for your industry, be sure to ask other companies (non-competitors) that serve the same industry. Find out where the best trade shows are, which organizations to join, how your target clients are involved in the industry and the community. Carefully research all of the advertising vehicles and call the current advertisers to ask how they are doing in the publication and how much they are paying for each ad.

Be prepared to test new tactics within each year's marketing plan. Test different offers within your direct mail campaigns, different approaches to trade shows, and different testimonials within your marketing collateral. Gather data on each of the variables to see which combinations perform best. This data will assist you in formulating your marketing plan for the following year. Testing consistently and effectively with each of your marketing tactics will become the basis of Formula Marketing. We will discuss "testing" in more detail in a later chapter.

Once you have your tactics developed, you will need to put them all into your marketing calendar and into your marketing budget.

Marketing Calendar:

The marketing calendar should be posted on your wall, with all of the implementation and event dates clearly listed for easy reference. Everyone within the company should receive a copy of the marketing calendar, with the obligation of signing an agreement not to share it with anyone outside your organization. As you develop your marketing calendar, you may identify conflicts that will cause you to modify your tactics. This is expected and helps you keep your marketing plan viable. You may also see gaps in your calendar, where you are not reaching out to your customers, training your sales staff, or maintaining your presence in the marketplace.

Your marketing calendar is a critical part of your marketing plan and operates as an extension of the Tactics section.

Marketing Budget:

Each of the tactics within your marketing plan should contain the estimated cost needed to carry out that tactic. By adding up the tactics, along with any other fixed marketing expenses, like personnel expenses, Yellow Page advertising, recurring printing costs, and corporate travel, you will have all of the line items needed to complete your marketing budget.

Percentage of Sales: Most companies determine their marketing budgets as a percentage of annual sales. Annual budget allocations for marketing typically range from 2% to 7% of total sales. So if your annual sales are $5,000,000, you would allocate $100,000 (2%) to $350,000 (7%). These allocations vary depending on your business.

If your business model is consumer driven, meaning you sell directly to consumers, a larger allocation will be needed. If your business serves other businesses, a smaller allocation is often sufficient.

It simply costs more money to reach consumers consistently and effectively than to reach businesses. This is true for a few reasons:

- A direct sales force can be leveraged to consistently reach business customers, and sales expenses are often divided into a separate budget category.
- Business-based businesses typically have higher average transaction amounts, so the desired sales volume is achieved with fewer total transactions.
- Consumers are protected by regulations that limit solicitations via telephone, canvassing, and direct mail.
- Consumer trends often change more quickly than trends within a business community.

Marketing budgets are most often allocated as a percentage of sales. This is a reliable method for setting aside dollars to maintain a consistent marketing presence. It becomes the foundation of formula marketing. However, there are circumstances in business that call for an alternative approach to allocating your marketing dollars.

Objective-Based Budgets: An objective-based budget is used when you want to hit a certain goal within a specified period of time. You may be ramping up your product line, entering a new market, increasing sales rapidly to capitalize on a fallen competitor, or growing your market share. In this form of budgeting, the objectives of your business will lead your marketing expenses rather than your annual sales.

For example, if you are launching a new business or business division and you have an objective of building sales to $500,000 within the first year, you will need to spend more capital upfront to build your brand, enter new markets, target new customers, and test your initial marketing plan. You will make more mistakes with your marketing plan, as your formula will not be built yet. Many of your tactics will be untested and will need to be refined over time. That means you will be spending more money to determine what works and what doesn't. Additionally, your new business or division will not have any annual sales yet, so allocating as a percentage of sales is impossible.

Another important advantage of an objective-based marketing plan is that your annual sales may not be growing at a rate that provides enough marketing dollars to grow your business.

If you want to double your sales next year, it is highly unlikely that an allocation of 5% of last year's sales will be sufficient to attain this goal. For this reason, Objective-Based Budgets are often more appropriate for a business.

Objective-Based Budgets are referred to as "Percentage of *Future* Sales", which simply means that you are allocating a percentage of the sales you want to have, vs. sales that you already have. So if you want sales of $1,000,000, you will allocate 5% of that figure, rather than your current sales of $500,000. You are effectively investing marketing dollars towards reaching your annual sales goal.

Marketing is an *Investment* not an Expense: Maintaining a marketing budget takes dedication, persistence and a great deal of faith. Marketing is expensive, so many companies do not set a formal marketing budget. They prefer to spend marketing dollars as they can afford them. For this reason, marketing budgets are often slashed in times of recession. This is exactly when marketing budgets should be increased. Your competitors are on the ropes, excess market share is available for the taking, and advertising and marketing costs are significantly lower – with rates reduced for advertising, trade shows, collateral materials, and personnel. However, many companies react to a recession or slow down by pulling in their marketing dollars, reducing their marketing staff, and cutting their advertising. By doing this, these companies are forfeiting market share to their competitors.

Whether in boom times or times of recession, marketing budgets must be viewed an as investment rather than an expense. Just as you invest in real estate or the stock market to grow your capital, investing marketing dollars into your business will yield a return. A diversified approach to investing has long been established as the best way to increase your personal net worth. In the same fashion, a diversified and balanced marketing matrix is the best way to grow your business. Viewing marketing as an investment will help you stay the course in the tough times. And, if you invest consistently, you will see a steady return on your investment. We will discuss marketing ROI in more detail in the next chapter.

As you can see, tactics are the lifeblood of any marketing plan and, for that reason, any marketing formula. However, they should not be deployed without taking the first three steps of (1) Situational Analysis, (2) Objectives, and (3) Strategies. The marketing calendar and marketing budget also must be fixtures within the tactics step. Finally, the Assessment step, Step 5 of the marketing plan, must not be skipped.

Step 5 - Assessment: What Worked?

Although it is very important, the assessment step is skipped in most marketing plans. This is often because marketing executives fail to build metrics into their marketing plans, so they are not able to properly assess or evaluate their results. As we discussed earlier, the key to formula marketing is establishing metrics to track the effectiveness of everything that you are doing. The assessment step is the process of reviewing your marketing results; whether they are sales figures, coupons redeemed, survey results, current market share figures, sales within certain products and services, and the metrics that assist you in evaluating overall company health.

You must have an assessment process built into your corporate marketing department in order to make adjustments for the future, optimize your tactics, modify your marketing message and capitalize on those tactics that are working. With a disciplined approach to marketing assessment, you will be able to develop a marketing formula that acts like an ATM machine, where you punch in a certain code and a specific amount of money will be generated. The assessment process is critical to building your marketing plan and developing a marketing formula.

Here are some of the items that could be part of your marketing assessment:

IV. Assessment
- Track Marketing Campaigns through Call Tracking Reports
- Track Visits to Website via Customized Landing Pages
- Track Click-Thrus and Open Rates on E-Blast Campaigns
- Track On-Line Surveys Completed
- Track Direct Mail Leads and Sales by Demographics / Zip Codes / Recipient Profiles, etc....
- Track Daily, Weekly, Monthly, Quarterly and Annual Sales
- Track Current Number of Corporate Customers
- Track Number of Transactions
- Track Average Transaction Amount
- Track Current Sales by Representative
- Track Number of Quotes by Sales Representative
- Track Outbound Calls by Sales Representative
- Track CRM activity by Sales Representative
- Track Sales within each Product and Service Offered by your Company
- Track Collateral Inventory
- Track Market Share within your Industry
- Track Coupon and Offer Redemption
- Track Version / Region / Segment Response
- Track Visits to your Business
- Track Volume of Calls / Visits / Clicks by Time and Day
- Track Leads and Sales Resulting Directly from Trade Shows
- Track Lead to "Close" Ratios
- Cost Per Lead by Tactic (you can break this down further, for example, by publication or advertising vehicle)
  - Cost per Sale by Tactic

And the list goes on. Everything within your business can be tracked, so long as you build the metrics and devices into each tactic up front.

The Marketing Dashboard: The key to Assessment is developing a grading system for each tactic, and ultimately each strategy, so you know when it is a success and when it is a failure. Combining all of this information into a few condensed reports allows you to see your performance in a given area at a glance. Many companies refer to synopses of these reports as a Marketing Dashboard.

Marketing Dashboard – Sample Company

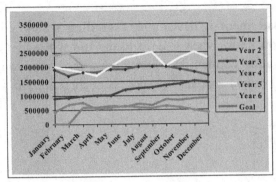

Monthly Sales

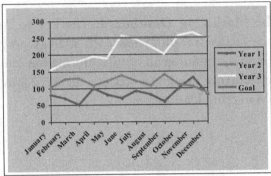

Average Transaction per Customer

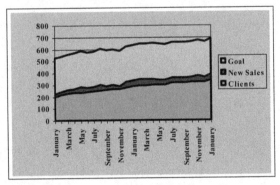

Cost Per Lead

New Customer Acquisition

Key Performance Indicators – Previous Month:

- Total Monthly Sales: $2,035,500
- Sales of New Service Y: $256,800
- Total Monthly Marketing Expense: $122,210
- Cost Per Lead: $905
- Lead-to-Sale Ratio: 35%
- Calls Generated from All Sources: 254
- Number of Active Customers: 367

- Sales of New Product X: $135,600
- Average Sales Per Rep: $84,600
- New Leads Generated: 135
- Cost Per New Customer: $2,600
- Total Website Visits: 1,469
- Average Transaction: $1,845
- Number of New Customers: 47

Just as a car's dashboard provides the driver with critical and timely performance information, a marketing dashboard allows you to review all of the data points to evaluate the performance of your marketing department. The car dashboard allows you to see the speed, gas mileage, gas inventory, oil pressure, and temperature. The same is true with a marketing dashboard.

A marketing dashboard can tell you the number of leads generated, the cost per lead, the closure ratio of leads, the profit margin per sale, the customer profile or source of sales, and many additional important details. All of this information from your dashboard can work together to give you a quick understanding of how the marketing department and marketing plan are performing. Over time, you can use your marketing dashboard to make efficient, unemotional decisions regarding your marketing plan.

The alternative to Assessment is expensive. You will not have a true understanding of what is working within your marketing plan. You may *think* you know what is working, but you will not know for certain until you study the numbers. That is the value of metrics assessment – the numbers don't lie. Without numbers, you may be spending thousands and thousands of dollars on areas that are not generating the best possible ROI.

ROI can be complicated. A given marketing tactic may generate hundreds of leads, but few sales. Or the sales it does generate may be low margin and undesirable. For example, direct mail may yield more leads than trade shows, but if your cost per sale for direct mail is 235% higher than the cost per sale for a trade show, you may want to modify your direct mail spend as compared to your trade show spend. This is just one scenario that would require study within the Assessment step. There are many, many more potential scenarios.

The unknown is what keeps marketing executives awake at night. You do not know what tactics work best until you try them. You may have optimized your website's Google ranking and ability to yield leads, but you won't know if trade publication advertisements will provide better qualified leads at a lower price until you test them. Trade publications, for example, may be the best possible place for you to advertise. But what if the design and copy within your ad campaign misses the mark with your target audience? There are so many variables to consider, that it is easy to make a critical mistake. These decisions have a significant impact on corporate sales and profits. No pressure!

Understanding your cost per sale, cost per lead, average transaction levels and other metrics derived from each tactic will assist you in making these key decisions. Testing and refining different marketing tactics will help you refine your marketing plan. You should always be testing new tactics, new offers, new photos and images, new headlines and tag lines, new demographics, new products, and new services. The Assessment step is the laboratory that will evaluate the effectiveness of each experiment.

All 5 steps of the marketing plan work in concert to yield a marketing formula. Your marketing formula should be simple, elegant and economically sustainable. We will explore the creation of your marketing formula in the next chapter.

CHAPTER 7:
OPTIMIZING YOUR MARKETING MATRIX

Once you have a marketing plan in place, and you have a process for evaluating your strategies and tactics within your assessment step, you will be able to determine which strategies and tactics belong in your marketing matrix.

What is a marketing matrix? It is the collection of proven strategies and tactics that work for your business. It is your "first string" of tactics; your top producers; your most reliable, get-it-done, you can count on a solid ROI, tactics. This is your marketing matrix.

The winning tactics will rise quickly to the top and you will know where the best return for your marketing dollars resides. With this data in hand, you will be able to optimize your marketing matrix, by selecting the top 4 to 6 marketing tactics that work for your business.

The optimized marketing matrix will form the core of your marketing formula. You should continue to test the offers, approaches and messages within your core matrix, and you should continue to test new tactics that are not part of these 4 to 6 tactics, but your work will be greatly simplified and your marketing dollars can be focused on those areas that work best for your business. In short, you will have your control group established within your marketing matrix.

It has been a while since we all entered our projects into the sixth grade science fair. However, I imagine you remember the basics of a science experiment. Within every science experiment, it is critical to have a control group, whether they are little plants in white Styrofoam cups, mice left unmolested in a cage, or, for the more advanced scientists in our classes, circuit boards within an anti-static chamber. The control group allows you to see improvement or decline within your other experiment groups.

The same principal works in marketing. Once you have your marketing matrix established, you are able to quickly evaluate any new strategies or tactics that you introduce. You will have a baseline established. Then you can simply plug the numbers of your new tactics into the assessment and see how they stack up to your marketing matrix.

Here's an example of an optimized marketing matrix for a regional insurance company:

Marketing Matrix: Guardian Insurance, Inc.

Tactic One: Direct Mail Newsletter to Customer Database
Budget: **Completion Date:** 10th of each Month
Printing & Mailing: $6,000
Less Corporate Co-Op Dollars @ 50%: <$3,000>
Total: $3,000
Note: Co-Op Dollars are marketing funds available from key suppliers or corporate partners

Tactic Two: Customer Referral Program: $500 for any referral paid to current client when a new client signs up. Details explained in a 4-page 8.5X5.5 brochure with testimonials, printed referral cards provided to current clients, promoted in newsletter, and discussed consistently in meetings.
Annual Budget: **Completion Date:** On-going
Brochures: $3,500
Referral Cards: $250
Referral Fees: $12,500
Newsletter: $00 – allocated in Tactic One
Total: $16,250

Tactic Three: Chamber of Commerce Membership and Sponsorships. Host several meetings per year, displaying company banner, staffed information table, distribute newsletters and promotional items (pens, letter openers, magnets) and business cards at the event. Provide 5-minute insurance update prior to guest speaker at every event, in exchange for sponsorship dollars. Always ask for referrals from group.
Annual Budget: **Completion Date:** On-going
Sponsorships and Donations to Chamber: $7,500
Information Table Staffing: $1,200
Collateral Materials: $00 – provided by national companies and Tactic One and Four
Promotional Items (pens/letter openers / magnets): $2,400
Event Banners: $600
Newsletters: $00 – allocated in Tactic One
SubTotal: $11,700
Less Corporate Co-Op Dollars @ 50%: <$5,850>
Total: $5,850

Tactic Four: Direct mail campaign to target customers using acquired direct mail list, using current customer profile and selected zip codes and demographics.

Annual Budget: **Completion Date:** 20th of every month
Purchased List: $250
Direct Mail Postcards (9X6): $3,000
Mail Services & Postage: $18,600
SubTotal: $21,850
Less Corporate Co-Op Dollars @ 50%: <$10,925>
Total: $10,925

Tactic Five: Monthly Inserts into local Newspapers, with overrun postcards from above.
Budget: **Completion Date:** 1st of every month
Daily Morning Star: $8,000
Weekly Clarion: $6,000
Monthly Sun Times: $2,500
Postcard Inserts: $00 – allocated in Tactic Four
SubTotal: $16,500
Less Corporate Co-Op Dollars @ 50%: <$8,250>
Total: $8,250

Tactic Six: Monthly Press Releases / Articles in local newspapers, as part of a special agreement, in the same ones that this insurance company advertises with. Add press releases to Monthly Newsletter.
Budget: **Completion Date:** 1st of every month
Staff to Write Press Releases: $1,200
Total: $1,200

Annual Marketing Budget - Grand Total: $45,475
(or $3,790 per month)

This is an example of the marketing matrix. It is a simple marketing formula for success that could be used by a regional insurance company, or your company with a few variations. These tactics are just examples, but they could work well for your business.

A few things to notice about the matrix above:

(1) The Tactics Work in Concert: Each of the tactics within this matrix work together to support one another. The newsletter used in Tactic One is also used in Tactic Two, Tactic Three, and Tactic Six. The Postcards in Tactic Four are used in Tactic Three and Five, and leveraged for free press coverage in Tactic Six. This is possible only when you have a consistent marketing matrix. You will quickly identify ways to weave your tactics together in harmony.

(2) **The Tactics Build The Company Brand:** This approach will assist you in building and maintaining a corporate brand. The marketplace will understand your messaging, which should be used consistently across all of the tactics within your marketing matrix.

(3) **Results:** A consistent marketing matrix, with a series of monthly tactics, will maintain consistent reach and frequency. (Time for a quick definition. *Reach* refers to how many people your marketing message is reaching, while *frequency* refers to how often those target individuals are receiving the message. Reach and Frequency are important factors within any advertising or marketing campaign.) A marketing matrix with consistent reach and frequency will provide a steady source of leads and sales. Metrics must be added to each of the elements within your marketing matrix so you can easily track your results.

(4) **The Tactics Work Together to Save Money:** Notice the co-op dollars applied to several of the tactics above. Not every business is able to leverage their marketing plans with co-op dollars, but with some creativity and determination you can partner with your suppliers, other regional businesses, and your shopping center to bring down the cost of your marketing. Also, notice how the postcards are used in the direct mail campaign, as inserts in the newspapers, and as collateral pieces at the Chamber of Commerce events. This brings the unit price down dramatically on the postcards, while boosting the leads derived from them.

The marketing matrix is a powerful force for your business. Once you have established your marketing matrix, you will have solved many of the mysteries of marketing. You no longer have to spend thousands of dollars to learn what works and what doesn't. You will invest your time more wisely as well, by focusing on your core marketing initiatives that drive the best results. You will also be able to project your ROI *before* you invest your marketing dollars, because you will have several months of data that show the average sales that are derived from each tactic, and the margins for those sales. You will no longer view your marketing department as a "black hole" of expenses, but as the revenue-producing core of your business. A well-designed marketing matrix will not only save your company money, but it will generate a steady stream of revenue and, therefore, profits.

So how do you build a marketing matrix?

Every company is different. Some companies arrive at their marketing matrix quickly, while it will take other companies several years to do so. Experience helps. Research is very beneficial. Boldness can pay dividends. And luck is frequently a key ingredient.

You will save a lot of money if you can build a successful marketing matrix quickly. So here are a few tips that may help you accelerate your progress:

- **Study the Marketplace:** Before you select your advertising tactics, take some time to study the marketplace. See what is going on. Most people have caught on to the fact that the Internet is exploding. How can you successfully leverage the web for your business? What are the hot trends? What is catching on and what is fading out? Notice things. Read magazines. Watch television and study the ads. Look at billboards. Analyze the direct mail pieces that you receive. Study the e-blasts that hit your inbox. Ask your friends and contacts for suggestions. Ask yourself what catches your own eye. What images resonate with you? What compels you to make a decision?

- **Read Industry Journals and/or Websites:** What is the industry telling you? How are businesses within your category marketing themselves in other parts of the country? Locally? Read the trade journals, attend the conferences and search the web to see how other companies within your industry are marketing their businesses. Pick up the phone and call some of the businesses within your industry that don't compete with you directly. They could be leveraging a direct sales force, distribute gifts to their top and target customers, or asking their best customers for referrals. Maybe they have a fleet of cars, trucks or vans that are wrapped or tagged with their logo and contact information. Perhaps they have a sophisticated direct mail and e-blast strategy. They might host a series of webinars, seminars, or lunch-and-learns.

- **Ask Your Customers:** Before you spend any money on advertising or marketing, ask your customers a few simple questions. Where do they learn about new businesses? What publications do they read? Where do they get their coupons? Do they use the Yellow Pages or the Internet? Where else do they shop? Do they like special offers? Do they rely on direct mail? Which television programs are they watching? Where do they get their news?

- **Study Your Competition:** Be careful with this one, as some of your direct competitors might not have any idea what they are doing. They could be making all of the classic marketing mistakes. However, chances are that they are doing a few things right. Study your competition's moves. Where do they advertise? What marketing tactics have worked for them? Ask your employees who once worked for a competitor, what marketing initiatives seemed to work well. Ask the customers of your competitors how they learned about them and why they decided to do business with them.

- **Ask Other Local Businesses:** Whether they are in your shopping center, your building, or your Chamber of Commerce, learn where other businesses in the marketplace are finding their customers. They may use a weekly shopper, register tape coupons, billboards, or radio. They may rely on word-of-mouth, a sophisticated referral program, public relations or door hangers. They may have an aggressive social media strategy, use Google analytics, advanced SEO (search engine optimization) or cable advertising. There is a wealth of information within your own backyard.

- **Publication Advertisers:** Call the business owners that advertise in specific publications within your local market or the trade journals for your industry. Ask them if they get a lot of leads from that publication. Would they advertise in the publication again? How much did they pay for their advertising? Was PR or an article included in the contract? Ask them how long they have been in business. Do they have a proven marketing matrix? Where else do they advertise? What works best for them?

- **Famous Local Companies:** You know who they are. The top car dealerships, furniture companies, restaurants, and local attractions. These local companies are famous and they advertise in all the right places. Call them and ask to speak with their marketing manager. Find out who they use for their direct mail and printing. Ask where most of their customers are coming from? See if they will share their marketing matrix with you. Ask them what made them famous and how much they spend on marketing annually. Ask the marketing manager if he or she will freelance on the weekends to help you build your marketing matrix.

- **Hire a Professional:** Whether you hire a marketing manager or savvy VP, an hourly consultant, or an agency, these professionals will help you take money-saving short-cuts in building your marketing matrix. They have done this before. They are experienced. Ask for their credentials. Ask for referrals from their current and former clients. Don't just hire a recent graduate from college to do this work for you. While they may make a great addition to your marketing department, in most cases they will not have the experience to help you take the short cuts needed to accelerate the development of your marketing matrix. Spend hundreds to save thousands. Bring in a hired gun to help you build your marketing formula, then turn over the daily operation and assessment to your in-house marketing team. This investment will pay dividends.

- **Co-Op Dollars and Partners:** Asking your suppliers, partners and industry connections for co-op dollars will bolster your marketing budget, just like the example of the insurance company in the beginning of this chapter. They effectively doubled their marketing budget through co-op dollars. These co-op partners also have a terrific understanding of what works and what doesn't. Rely on their industry-wide knowledge and ask many questions. You will learn a great deal from them.

- **Trial and Error:** It is inevitable. You will eventually have to try a few things. Some will work. Some will not. Do not consider the initiatives that don't work "failures". Rather, you have invested in testing these approaches and are now able to rule them out of the marketing matrix. Keep good notes and records. Knowing what has worked and not worked in the past is very valuable to you in future years, with future marketing staff members. This information will also be extremely valuable to anyone who wishes to purchase your business and the addition of your marketing files in the transaction will help you in the final negotiations.

Following through with these recommendations will save you thousands of dollars and a great deal of time. For all of these time- and money-saving tips, there is an equally important list. The list of what not to do.

What Not To Do:

- **Don't Choose Something Just Because *You* Like It:** You are not the customer. Just because you are involved in little league baseball, does not mean that your customer is. By the same token, just because you throw all of your direct mail away doesn't mean that your customers do. Direct mail has been proven to be one of the most powerful forms of marketing and can be terrific at generating an immediate response. So don't rule it out because you are worried about the environment. Rather, seek to create a "green" mailer. Many business owners make the mistake of assuming they are their own customer. One of my clients owns a greeting card company. He is fully aware that he is not his own customer, but his wife and her friends most definitely are. For this reason, he relies on his core demographic to make his most important marketing decisions. He understands that he is not the right person to determine which new greeting cards to launch, which ones to phase out, where to market his product, and how to design his image and brand.

- **Don't Single Trial:** Don't ever try something once and then decide if it works or not. Marketing requires repetition (Frequency) to work. You will rarely hit a winner on the first, second, or even third try. Don't imagine that you are saving money when you sign a short-term contract. You are more likely wasting money by not fully evaluating whether the tactic works or not. You must build frequency for your message to gain a response. The consumer needs to see your same message in the same place three to seven times before it resonates. Statistics suggest it takes three times to "see" a message and seven times to "respond" to a message. Don't take short cuts here. You will save money in the long run by investing more upfront.

- **Don't Believe Every Advertising Sales Reps:** I have a great fondness for advertising sales reps. In fact, I have sold advertising in my own publication for several years. Most sales reps are focused on their commission, not on your success. Do not take their claims at face value, but research them carefully to confirm that they are true. If your advertising sales rep is young, attractive, well dressed and smooth in their approach, they might not have any understanding of your business, your customer, or your industry. Do not rely on these people to make your marketing decisions. Leverage their knowledge in other ways (like which advertisers do best with their vehicle, what offers work, where are the deals in their product, and the best placements / time-slots). Do your research, and then make an independent marketing decision.

- **Don't Do Something Because it is Inexpensive:** This is very common. "Well, it was so cheap, I just had to give it a try." Maybe, but you get what you pay for. In many cases, these inexpensive forms of marketing and advertising are a waste of money. You have your image to consider, after all. You may not want your company to be seen in something that is considered "cheap" by your target customer.

- **Don't Do Something that is too Expensive to Sustain:** The all or nothing, big splash on Super Bowl Sunday is a poor strategy for most businesses. The key to successful marketing is being consistent. Don't put all of your marketing eggs into a single basket, especially if you can't continue to afford that tactic. In most cases, you will be wasting your money. Frequency is critical to successful marketing. Save your marketing dollars to fight another day and in another way.

- **Don't Do Something Because You have Always Done it that Way:** Times change. Trends change. Tastes change. Customers move (approx. 20% of consumers move to a new home each year and turn over in business is even higher). Target customers may become younger and rely on new techniques to make their decisions. You need to adapt to these changes and try new things. Otherwise, your marketing matrix may become obsolete.

- **Don't Eliminate Something Because You have Tried it Before:** Same as above. Just because it didn't work three years ago does not mean that it will not work today. Maybe your ad campaign was not effective, or your offers were not strong enough to drive a good response. If it is working for other businesses, it may work well for you. Do your research carefully and, if it looks promising, consider testing it.

Developing an effective marketing matrix takes an investment of time and money. These investments will pay dividends if you remain committed to a consistent approach. In order to develop your marketing matrix, it is necessary to test and refine your tactics and strategies. Over time, with consistent testing and refinements, you will build a highly efficient, cost-effective marketing formula that works.

Start simply. Choose five or six marketing tactics that address your Situational Analysis, can help you achieve your Objectives, and are aligned with your Strategies. Continue to use those five or six core tactics to form the foundation of your marketing matrix. Be consistent with them, improve them through trial-and-error, refine the offers and calls-to-action, test different approaches and campaigns within your core matrix. However, it is critical to keep your core marketing matrix in tact.

For example, a care dealership might have a marketing matrix that looks like this:

Marketing Matrix: Care Dealership
Tactic One: Radio, TV & Cable Advertising
Tactic Two: Direct Mail to Customer List and Target Profile
Tactic Three: Customer Referral Program
Tactic Four: Special Weekend Sales Promotions
Tactic Five: Internal Sales Promotions

While a Dry Cleaning Company might have a matrix that looks like this:

Marketing Matrix: Dry Cleaner
Tactic One: Shopping Center Advertising (register tape coupons, shopping cart advertising, signage, flyers at other businesses within shopping center)
Tactic Two: Direct Mail to Customer Database
Tactic Three: Inserts in Local Publications
Tactic Four: Door Hangers and Direct Mail to Homes within a 2-mile radius
Tactic Five: Bounce-Back Coupons and VIP Customer Club

Both businesses will try other tactics, but the five core tactics will form the foundation of their marketing matrix.

Now it's your turn. Take a moment to jot down the five or six tactics that could comprise your marketing matrix. What are they now? What would they be? How would you use them? Be sure they are aligned with your Situational Analysis, Objectives, and Strategies. Then put them on paper. Begin to research each of them and run them by people whom you trust, people in the know, other business owners, your current customers, and gifted marketers. Please do this now. The book will wait for you.

Your Marketing Matrix

Tactic One:

Tactic Two:

Tactic Three:

Tactic Four:

Tactic Five:

That wasn't so hard, was it? This could be the core of your future marketing matrix. You have some work to do to confirm that this is the correct matrix, but you have started the process - a process that will make your business more profitable.

Once you have a reliable marketing matrix, you can then "test" new tactics alongside your proven tactics to see if you are able to yield any improvements and are able to promote the most successful new tactics to the first-string. Continue to do this through the life of your business. You will have your core matrix, and the best of the new tactics in test mode. This approach will help you grow your business, increase your profits, and improve your margins.

In short, an effective marketing matrix should be one of the most important things that you do for your business. It is foundational to Formula Marketing.

What is Formula Marketing? It is building a marketing matrix that yields a consistent profit. It is designing a marketing matrix that provides strong results. It is creating a marketing matrix that does not surprise you, but provides a steady stream of new customers, repeat visits, and repeat sales. Formula Marketing is successfully building a marketing matrix that is tied to the five steps of your marketing plan:

(1) Situational Analysis
(2) Objectives
(3) Strategies
(4) Tactics
(5) Assessment

In Formula Marketing, you will know that your annual marketing investment of, for example, $148,950 dollars will yield annual sales of $2,325,000, a gross profit of $430,500, and a net profit of $225,895. Or figures like these. Formula Marketing provides you with growth, consistent sales, and consistent profits. It may look like magic, but it is a science. Formula Marketing is a science worth investing in.

CHAPTER 8:
YOUR CORPORATE BRAND

We have devoted the last few chapters to creating a marketing plan and a marketing matrix, which make up the core of your marketing formula. However, your formula isn't finished yet.

Your corporate brand is a very important part of formula marketing. But what exactly is a corporate brand?

It is more than a logo. It is more than a mission statement. It is more than a tagline or corporate colors. It is the combination of all of these things, and more, that create your corporate brand.

Your corporate brand is essentially the story of your company. Everyone loves a story. You need to tell your company story clearly and concisely. If you do not write your story, someone else with will write it for you. The following is a short-list of some of the ingredients of a corporate brand:

Logo: A good company logo will convey the essence of the brand in a single image. It will usually represent the company identity, colors and personality in a summarized, often iconic, conclusion of design. It will often be recognizable, unforgettable, and bold. Think of the logos of the companies that you respect. What comes to mind? Do you think of Coke, McDonalds, Travelers, H&R Block, NBC, Ralph Lauren, Nike, or IBM? Or do you prefer Pepsi, Applebee's, Google, ESPN, Intel, Tommy Bahama, Vans, or Apple? Or do you relate more to Monster, Starbucks, YouTube, Hollister, Cobian and Asus?

Each of these logos appeal to a different customer. They stand for different things. They convey different meanings, evoke different emotions and connotations, and capitalize on different behaviors. They stand boldly for the company behind them, the special people involved, the unique processes deployed, and the experience the customer will have in the use of the products and services.

If a logo is at odds with the core customer, out of step with the company identity, or out of touch with the company offerings, it lacks the power of conviction to compel the consumer to invest in that logo and the company behind it. A logo must have integrity. A logo must stand for something. A logo must be the heartbeat of a company.

For example, if a financial services firm has a bouncy, candy-colored logo that emphasizes fun, whimsy and creative irreverence, the serious investor or high net worth individual will most likely stay away. By that same token, if a toy store adopts a stark, buttoned down, monochromatic logo, it will fail to resonate with its young customers.

Developing a logo isn't easy. It is rare to pay a graphic designer $35 to develop a logo as powerful and iconic as the Nike swoosh. I once had a client contact me on a Thursday afternoon, requesting a finished logo by Monday morning. I had no experience with the company, had never visited their offices, was unaware of their services, and did not know the profile of their core customers. To make a long story short, the logo was not completed in a weekend. A gifted brand designer was hired and, over a few weeks, the logo concept evolved.

In developing a good logo, a company should begin with the tastes and perspectives of their target customers, go deep into the corporate culture, soar over their products and services, and land with a brand that stands apart from the clutter of the marketplace.

Colors: Colors also define a company brand. The consistent use of red, blue, white, and green will serve to define a company's brand. The brand is also shaped by the tone of the colors, the shades, the brush strokes and the composition. Consider that both the Starbucks logo and the Monster drink logo are green. But the colors are completely different shades and positioned in different ways to convey the brand. Company colors must be consistent with the identity, appealing to the target customers, and sustainable throughout the company's collateral materials, website, business cards, and logo.

Design Themes, Fonts and Elements: Company brands are infused with consistent fonts, positioning, orientations, and uses. They are supported by design themes that consistently convey the experience of doing business with that company. The design elements provide familiarity with each new transaction, and convey an image that encourages referrals.

Images: The photos, illustrations, and designs must connect with the customers, quickly convey the services, and encapsulate the promised experience. They must be believable, tie to the heart strings, and allow the consumer to quickly trust. They must appeal to the core demographics, match up with the price points, and accelerate the messaging.

Taglines: A tagline often accompanies the company logo, but it should be able to stand alone, too. It is your elevator speech, a synopsis of your services, and a definition of your purpose. Taglines can be changed to reflect your changing product line, and launched with a new campaign. They say things like "Just Do It", "Fly the Friendly Skies", "Your Home Office" and "Relax". They offer the conclusion to the transaction, the result of the investment, and can be written in the postcard home in future referrals.

Products and Services: What you sell reflects who you are. I am not aware of any uptight companies that sell fly-fishing gear. I have never seen a laid-back, come-what may company successfully handle consumer finances. It is rare to see a serious, no-nonsense theme park. The products and services offered by a company will define that company. They are foundational in the brand.

Corporate Dress and Uniforms: How the people dress within a company makes a statement of what is valued. Whether the company values are leisure, rebellion, attention to detail, or delicious food, the dress of the employees crafts the customer's experience and expectations and further defines the brand.

Design of Retail Locations: Not every business has a retail location, but those that do need to consider their brand as they design the tenant improvements, the shape of the counters, the lighting, position of the logo, and flow of commerce. It is important to ask "Why are the customers here?" Are they in a hurry, just want to get things done, needing a break, or ready for some serious fun? The décor should permit them to realize their hoped-for experience.

Packaging: The packaging used in products and services should operate like a company retail location. It should provide an experience as the package is opened, and promote the unique features within the product. It should be consistent with the tastes of the core demographic, and encourage purchase from the shelf.

Website: Increasingly, websites are the retail locations we visit most. Transactions are rising quickly and society is increasingly comfortable with shopping online. A company's website should feature the benefits of the company brand. Depending on the company, a website can convey an easy flow, a data rich environment, a few core choices, or a huge variety. It can evoke a simple, sleek, meditative state. Or it can offer the jumble and excitement of an ancient, open marketplace. The structure of the site must resonate with the core demographics of the target customer and convey the corporate brand in a fashion consistent with the logo, the products and services, and the company colors.

Mission Statement: I believe that most mission statements are too long and too similar to every other company's mission statement. A good mission statement should be short enough that the company employees can remember it, like "quality is job one" or "doing what we do best". A mission statement rarely doubles as a tagline, but it should come close to doing so. It should be outward facing and appropriate for customer consumption. It should define the corporate culture and deliver a promise to the marketplace. It should remind employees why they were hired, and reinforce a customer's decision.

Business Systems and Processes: How is business done? Whether always delivered on-time, slow-cooked, engineered with precision, baked with love, flawlessly executed, environmentally friendly, built to last, or earned over time, the processes and systems deliver more than just the products and services. They deliver the brand. How you make something is a story worth telling and should be incorporated into your brand. Whether you let your customers tell the story through testimonials (which is extremely powerful), or you chronicle your unique approach yourself, the engine of your business should be shared. How you do things should be central to your corporate brand.

Corporate Identity: Who are you? What do you stand for? What makes you different? Who works at the company? Who are your customers? How do you do things? How can you help someone? All of these things make up your corporate identity. They need to be infused into your corporate brand in a consistent and meaningful way.

Collateral: The materials you print, the forms you use, the literature you distribute, the flyers you pass out, the pieces that you mail, and the presentation folders that you deliver should consistently convey your corporate brand. I have seen many carefully established brands destroyed in seconds with a cheap, poorly designed sell sheet. Do not let your collateral diminish your brand. Spend the extra money and invest the additional time required to present your message and company brand in a professional and consistent fashion.

Marketing Matrix: Finally, the marketing matrix of a company should be precisely aligned with its brand. The strategies and tactics deployed by a company must help to build the brand. A Mercedes Benz dealer should not advertise in the PennySaver, and Chuckie Cheese should not be a corporate sponsor of 60 Minutes. How you promote your brand should be consistent with that brand. If you are a high-end pool builder, you should advertise in the most respected luxury home improvement magazines in town. If you are a high-volume car wash, then advertising in ValPak should work well. If you are a brand-centric real estate company, you should have a highly-trained and professional sales force. Your marketing matrix must resonate with your customers and your corporate brand in order to be effective.

I have covered these items in some detail because they are important in establishing your company brand. Hopefully, you will look at your company brand more comprehensively. This is not a complete list, but all of these items are core to a brand.

Your company brand is key to Formula Marketing. It is an essential part of the formula. Your brand must be consistent with your company philosophy and the methods you use to share your story. As a result, many companies create brand standards and brand centers to protect their brands.

Brand Standards: What are brand standards? They are the rules, regulations, guidelines and suggestions for the use of the corporate logo, taglines, colors, fonts and images. The brand standards should be maintained by the marketing department and communicated through the entire organization. They should be shared with partners and vendors, like the commercial packaging and printing companies the firm works with.

The brand standards should anticipate the corporate brand's travels through the marketplace. For example, when a red and blue logo is to be printed in black, what elements will be changed? How will the company name be typed into a document, where it is inappropriate to place the logo? How will the company name appear? What if the logo needs to be printed vertically, to be placed on a banner or a promotional pen, will the tagline be altered? When can the tagline be separate from the logo, and when can the tagline stand alone?

As you can see, there will be many questions regarding the use of your brand and logo. It is important to answer those questions within your brand standards. Many companies create and host Brand Centers online, allowing access to company staff members, vendors and partners. Within the Brand Center, the rules and regulations for use of the logo and other brand elements are clearly stated. Examples are displayed, showing correct and incorrect uses of the logo and brand in a wide variety of placements. The Brand Center can also have a section that explains the importance of the brand, the choice of colors, the meaning behind the tagline, and the symbolism of the logo.

Once the brand standards are established and communicated, they must be enforced. Not on penalty of death, but it must be understood that the correct use of the company brand and logo is a critical part of the marketing formula. It is important to protect the corporate brand so that it may endure, inspire, and build trust with the consumer.

For example, a prestigious automobile brand could be the main sponsor of a golf tournament and, as part of the sponsorship package, they host a hospitality tent, post banners throughout the event, park their cars near the tee boxes and pass out complimentary water bottles to the players and attendees. The whole event can look extremely professional and precise, which is aligned with the carmaker's brand.

The car company is careful to make sure that the same logo and tagline used on the banners and signs is used in the television spots. The logo on the water bottles matches the logo and design used within the e-blast campaign sent to the ticket holders. The shirts of the staff in the hospitality tent match the shirts of the staff supporting the vehicle demonstrations throughout the event. The tickets, programs, event agenda, and media booth all have a consistent look and feel. In effect, the auto company will be proving their brand, with flawless execution throughout the event.

Imagine if, in this scenario, the printer that creates the banners uses the wrong logo color, so all of the banners do not match the rest of the branded pieces. What if the labels on the water bottles used the logo design from three years ago, rather than the current presentation? What if the staff members decided not to wear their event logo shirts, and wore their everyday clothes? What if one of the words in the tagline is misspelled on the program cover? All of these transgressions of the brand would work together to minimize the company brand and diminish the event sponsorship.

The same holds true for your company. The brand used on your letterhead and business cards should be in sync with the brand conveyed on your trucks. Your direct mail pieces should be consistent with the use of your brand in your trade show materials. Your e-blast campaigns should support the branding of your website. The logo used on your promotional items (pens, stress balls, letter openers, and mini-calculators) should follow the same standards as your brochures, sales sheets, and presentation folders.

Coordinating a consistent use of your brand sounds easy. However, it becomes increasingly complicated when your company has offices across the country, franchisees in different markets, 8 people within the marketing department, a sales team of 65 people, 12 different print vendors, and various outsourced partners that handle your company's SEO, website, LSM (local store marketing), and direct mail programs.

If you have clearly stated and consistently communicated brand standards, you will be able to coordinate your brand consistently. However, without brand standards, chaos will reign and your brand equity, in which you have invested significant dollars, could be diminished.

Remember, it all comes back to the formula. If you put the work in up front to establish your brand standards, create your marketing plan, select your marketing matrix and invest in the autonomy and ROI responsibilities of your marketing department, your formula will reap great dividends and can be maintained with little effort. However, if you run your marketing department with a series of reactive marketing initiatives, create campaigns by the seat of your pants, fail to test and refine your tactics, and procrastinate on the management of your brand, your marketing department will likely do more harm than good.

If the chaos scenario describes your company, please don't lose heart. The fact is, chaos describes the majority of companies. Few companies, especially small businesses, execute formula marketing correctly. It takes understanding, experience, resources, faith, and an investment of time. Formula marketing has been mostly reserved for the wealthy, powerful corporations. However, this does not have to be the case. The same principles that are used by the mega, brand-conscious corporations, can be used by your business. That is the point of this book. That has been the message within these initial chapters. You can do this, too. You can use formula marketing within your business. And the steps are not complicated or terribly expensive. In fact, formula marketing is the most cost-effective approach for marketing your business.

To emphasize this point, let's summarize the elements of formula marketing that have been covered within this book.

The Formula Marketing Summary:
(1) Clearly Empower your Marketing Staff and Give Them Complete Authority
(2) Establish ROI Expectations for your Marketing Department
(3) Establish your Marketing Metrics
(4) Define Your Customer
(5) Differentiate Your Company
(6) Write Your Marketing Plan
  - Situational Analysis
  - Objectives
  - Strategies
  - Tactics (Test Constantly)
  - Assessment
(7) Create Your Marketing Calendar
(8) Develop Your Marketing Budget
(9) Create Your Marketing Matrix
(10) Establish Brand Standards

This is a simple list. It has been de-mystified in the earlier pages of this book. Put this summary on your bulletin board, discuss it at your next company meeting, and begin to infuse it into your corporate culture.

Formula marketing works. The alternative can be extremely expensive and destructive to your business. Follow these 10 steps and you will reap tremendous rewards, greater sales, and improved profits.

We have now delivered on the promise provided in the title of the book. We have explained the concept of Formula Marketing. While we are not finished with underscoring and developing the concept, we have covered the foundation.

In the following chapters, we are going to cover some of the ins and outs, insider perspectives, and details of operating Formula Marketing. There will be several tricks and tips that you can use in your business. These ideas and tactics have been developed by hundreds of gifted marketing professionals and implemented effectively within their marketing plans. Pick and choose the ones that will work best for your business and add them to your tactics.

In the chapters ahead, we will be departing from the Formula Marketing strategy and moving into the tactics that can be used to execute this strategy.

Chapter 9:
Advertising Tips

Advertising is an investment, not an expense. This is a critical perspective to adopt, because advertising is expensive. It requires a leap of faith to put thousands of dollars into an advertising campaign or vehicle. Real estate, stocks, and college tuition are also expensive, but we recognize readily that they are investments, rather than expenses. If you invest wisely, each will pay a return and will increase your equity position. The same is true with advertising.

As you invest in advertising, there are ways to save money that will help you boost your ROI. There are many terrific books on advertising and marketing that offer ideas for maximizing your investment dollars and saving money on your marketing tactics. If you study these books, you will literally save your company thousands of dollars on advertising and marketing each year. Some of my favorite books for advertising on a shoe-string budget are the *Guerilla Marketing* series by Jay Conrad Levinson. I have met Mr. Levinson on a few occasions and hired him to speak at corporate conventions. His ideas for saving money and getting the most from your ad buys are a must-read for any marketing professional or small business owner.

In this chapter, I will cover a few of the techniques that I have used to stretch my marketing budget and boost company sales. This chapter will not be comprehensive. For every one idea provided here, there are hundreds of money-saving advertising tips available. The purpose of this chapter is to share the possibilities that exist, so you can develop your own money-saving measures.

Never Pay Rate Card: Most advertising vehicles, such as radio, television, cable, Internet, newspapers, magazines, outdoor (billboards), and direct mail publications will have a rate card that lists their standard prices. It is best to view these rate card prices as guidelines only. You should never actually pay the rate card price. They are like the asking price for real estate or an automobile. You are expected to negotiate these purchases. The same is true with advertising. If a magazine charges $4,500 for a full-page, full-color advertisement on a long-term contract rate of 12 issues, so the total buy is $54,000, begin the negotiations at something south of a 40% discount, or $32,400 ($2,700 per issue). You may not receive this price, but it will give you a good opportunity to negotiate a substantial discount. The companies that own these advertising vehicles want to lock in cash flow and move their inventory. They will be interested in offering a discount to good, long-term advertisers who pay their bills on time.

Agency Discount: Advertising agencies typically receive a 15% discount for media buys, which they keep for their expertise and to cover the cost of their time. These discounts are standard for most advertising companies. You do not need to use an advertising agency to purchase your advertising, you can buy direct. (I want to be quick to say that a good media buyer or ad agency can save you a fortune and more than pay for themselves, so working with an agency can be a terrific money-saving strategy.) If you buy your advertising yourself, don't yield the agency discount. Form your own advertising agency that represents your company. If you have a restaurant called The Blue Ocean Café, consider forming an advertising agency called Blue Ocean Advertising. Set up a separate checking account for this business entity and purchase all of your advertising through your new in-house agency. You will receive this standard 15% discount, in addition to other negotiated discounts.

Frequency Discount: It is important to stay with a given advertising vehicle for the long-term to establish frequency with the consumer and thoroughly test the advertising vehicle as a tactic. You should not purchase a single issue, or just a few days of broadcast – this is a waste of money. You need to make long-term advertising commitments to ensure that your investments pay off. You will be rewarded for this strategy by the advertising companies, as they offer discounts for long-term buys. The more advertising you buy, the lower the price per issue or per spot. These are called frequency discounts. For example, a direct mail advertising publication may charge $3,000 for a single issue, $2,500 for 4 issues, and $2,000 for 12 issues. If you buy all of your advertising in long-term contracts, you will save a fortune over time. However, be sure to read every line of the advertising contract and eliminate clauses that charge big penalties for canceling your agreement early.

Payment Terms / Cash Up-Front: Advertising companies need to manage their cash flow, too. They will offer discounts if you are willing to pay up front for your advertising, or within 15 days, vs. 30 days. These cash discounts typically run at 2%, but ask for 5% and see what happens. The worst thing they can say is "No, we only offer a 2% discount for cash up front". These term-related discounts are available in many other areas as well, like printing, trade shows, promotional items, and other marketing expenses.

Trade: Many advertising companies are able to trade their services and products for yours. They may need or want your dry cleaning services, dentistry, restaurant meals, limousine service, pest control, home improvements, and other things that you have to offer. In exchange, they can lower your advertising rates or trade 100% of your buy. Trade is very common and popular, especially with local advertising companies. If you engage in trade, be sure to have a contract in place that states all of the terms of the trade. Also be sure to report the use of trade accurately for tax purposes.

Nice Guy Discount: Don't laugh! This really works. At the end of your negotiations, just before you are going to sign the agreement, ask for an additional 10% off. You can call this discount anything you like, but I have always referred to it as a "nice guy discount". I receive this additional 10% about half the time I ask.

Free Graphic Design or Production: It costs money to design your print advertisements or to produce your spots. The advertising companies often have a graphics design or production department that can produce your advertisements. Another way to negotiate a better price is to ask that they provide these services at no cost or at a deep discount. Once the artwork or production is completed, you will own the artwork – or at least you should. Make sure there is language in your agreement that gives you all of the rights to the creative, so you can use it in future advertising with other companies and vehicles. One caution – you get what you pay for. If you want to develop a professional and lasting brand, you will want to have your ads designed by a professional graphic designer or agency, rather than by the production staff within the media company. While these individuals are often very talented, they will be more focused on their specific slice of the media market, rather than on creating a consistent brand for your company. Rather, you may want to provide these media companies with your brand standards and your brand package of logos, images, fonts, and headlines and allow them to adapt your creative to their publication. This will allow you to save money, while maintaining the integrity of your brand.

Extra / Extra: In addition to the discounts mentioned above, the advertising companies are also able to provide other extras as part of your buy. You can request overruns of a printed piece (like direct mail postcards, circulars, or flyers) so you can use them as tradeshow sell sheets or inserts. You can request that these companies link to your website from their website to boost your SEO rankings, or offer special features or mentions of your business on their website. You can ask them to include your company in an article, promotional feature, or special interview with their news staff. You can request their best placement at no extra cost. You can pay for a black and white ad, and ask them to throw in 4-color for free. You can request a larger ad for the price of a smaller ad, and so on. The point here is everything is negotiable. It is often easy for these advertising companies to accommodate your requests, in exchange for a longer-term agreement and timely payment.

Co-Op Dollars: Beyond the discounts that could be available from the advertising companies, you can reduce your advertising costs by requesting or applying for co-op dollars from your key suppliers. Many national suppliers have these programs in place. It is very much to the benefit of your suppliers that you sell more of their product or service. They do not often have direct access to the consumer, so you represent the bridge to the consumer within a specific market. They are often very willing to share the cost of your advertising, as long as you feature their brand prominently within the advertising, within their stated brand standards. Be sure to receive their full approval in advance of signing your advertising contracts. This approval should include the creative, as well. In many cases, the supplier company will provide up to 50% of the cost of an advertising campaign in co-op dollars. Apply for these funds early in the year, or before the next year begins. There are other companies within your industry asking for the same funds. Be sure to apply before these funds are spent or allocated.

If your key suppliers do not have a formal co-op program, sit down with them and negotiate one. Show them your plans (but not all of the details, as they may work with your direct competitors) and your tracking systems to determine metrics for each campaign. Offer to share the results with them as part of the program. They will be interested in your survey results, leads, the performance of your offers, and the other details of your campaign results. They will take you seriously if you show them that you have an established marketing plan with metrics and assessment built in. This will help you a great deal as you negotiate your co-op dollars.

Strategic Partnerships: If you are unable to locate a source for co-op dollars, or you have already tapped these funds, consider forming strategic partnerships with other non-competing companies within your industry, the publications you advertise in, or your shopping center. These companies are often trying to reach the same customers, so work together to save money.

For example, you will often see a real estate company partnered with a mortgage company or appraiser. You may see the dry cleaners share their marketing expenses with a restaurant within the same shopping center. You may see two complementary technology firms sharing the expense of a trade show booth or a direct mail piece. Many commercial printers will formally refer work to graphic design firms, and vice versa. A window installation company can market its services along with a paint contractor or builder. A high-end, professional landscape company can form a strategic partnership with a residential pool builder. A home builder can market its services along with the regional bank that has a real estate construction lending division. An office cleaning service can market its services with a commercial plant care business, or an industrial supply company. A notary company can market its business through local banks that no longer offer notary services. An accounting company can refer trust work to a law firm that specializes in that discipline. Doctors can refer patients to massage therapists, pharmacies, or providers of alternative medicine or nutritional supplements. A car dealership can provide gift cards to local restaurants, car washes, or detailing services as a way to thank their customer for a recent purchase. And the list goes on.

Take a moment to jot down a list of businesses that could present strategic partnership opportunities. To get ideas, consider the businesses within your shopping center, within the publications that you advertise in, or within your local chamber of commerce. You will be surprised how many companies you can work with and how many strategic partnerships you can develop. Be sure to maintain the relationship, put your agreements in writing, and add these partnerships to your marketing plan and, over time, to your marketing matrix.

Marriage Mailers: Taking the strategic partnership one step further, you can work with your partners to produce a professional direct mail piece or newsletter and mail it out to an acquired direct mail list, or to each company's database. You can share the cost of printing and postage and, therefore, afford to mail the piece with greater frequency. You can offer tips and articles that will be interesting to your target customers, while featuring your services and the products of your strategic partner(s). Before you dive in, be sure to spend the extra time and money to design a professional piece that builds, rather than diminishes, your brand. Often in a co-op or strategic partnership arrangement, the combined marketing pieces look too cluttered and unprofessional. In design, less is more. Work together to hire a professional to handle the initial design or template, then begin your campaign.

Broker: Cal Worthington is famous for selling cars in Southern California. He and his dog, Spot, have sold millions of automobiles over the years. It is worth mentioning that Spot has been a tiger, a camel, and several other exotic animals – everything but a dog. That's part of the fun of his ads. While Cal Worthington comes across as a folksy, unsophisticated, and hokey used car salesman, he is actually closer to a marketing genius. Worthington began the practice of buying all of the commercials on late night television, then reselling the ads to other companies. He re-sold the ads at a markup sufficient to provide his own advertising for free. Through his own media buying company, Worthington successfully brokered enough advertising to get his campaign buys at little or no cost. Genius!

Why should Cal Worthington have all the fun? You can broker a direct mail newsletter for your shopping center or industry and mark-up the printing, postage and production to cover your individual costs. You can also control the placement of your ads, as Cal Worthington always did, so you receive the premier placements and spots. You can apply the same principle to tradeshows, promotions, sponsorships, media, printing, and other marketing activities. Just be careful to create professional marketing pieces that do not diminish your brand, or the brands of your strategic partners. Not only can you discount or cover many of your marketing costs, you could even turn this concept into a profit center.

Referral Programs and Discounts: With these same strategic partners, you can create referral programs that drive more business to one another's businesses. These arrangements can be casual networks, or formal programs. It is often difficult to track referrals, so add a special offer within the referral. For example, if a computer accessories store refers a customer to an IT professional, they could do so with a discount coupon that offers their customer 25% off their first purchase. The discount coupon would carry the computer store's logo and branding and say something like "A special offer for our best customers". This creates value to the coupon while adding a tracking component to the piece, and measurable results for the referral program. Customers will appreciate the savings, the strategic partner will appreciate the new business, and you will see positive reciprocation from both.

Better Postage Rates: Postage is expensive and it is difficult to keep pace with the changes and rates created by the USPS. It is a good idea to work with a professional mail house or mailing services company to secure the best possible postage rates. These services charge a few hundred dollars to process your direct mail campaigns, but they can save you many times that on your campaigns. Postage savings often begin with the design of your pieces. For example, the size of your direct mail piece will impact the cost of mailing it. By making your direct mail piece thinner, changing it to a postcard, or reducing the dimensions by an inch, you can dramatically reduce the cost of postage. There are also discounts for mailing pre-sorted mail, or selecting Standard Mail instead of First Class. Standard Mail takes longer to deliver, but the few extra days are often well worth the savings. There are also discounts for non-profit organizations. Additional discounts are available if you mail to a single or cluster of zip codes, or to a specific carrier route. It is very difficult to stay on top of the changing postal regulations, so work with an expert in this area. It will pay dividends and can reduce your cost of postage by as much as 50%.

Testimonials: It is important to use testimonials in your advertising and marketing campaigns. Whether you design the testimonials into your ad campaigns, or feature them on your website, the positive words of your current customers carry a great deal of weight with potential, new customers. Testimonials can form the basis of due diligence for a customer who is considering your business over your competitor.

Formalize the program by asking your customers for testimonials. Receive their permission to reprint their kind words and use them on your website, collateral, and ad campaigns. People are busy, so it is helpful to take the essence of what they have said about your business either verbally or within their e-mails and type up a crisp, positive testimonial that captures their expressed sentiments. Then ask them personally if they would be willing to provide a testimonial like the sample you have provided. They will often give you permission to use the sample, or they will use what you have provided as a guideline to write their own testimonial. Be sure to disclose to your customers that you plan to use their testimonials within your marketing campaigns and require their written permission or a signed release to do so.

   If you are not sure of the effectiveness of testimonials, test them out within your next ad campaign. For example, if you have a direct mail program to 10,000 home owners, include your call tracking, coupon redemption, and response tracking mechanisms and print two versions of your direct mail pieces; 5,000 direct mail pieces will prominently feature the testimonial, while 5,000 will not have the testimonial. It is critical to make sure that everything else about the direct mail pieces is identical. It is most effective to test a single variable at a time. Do not include different offers, designs, zip codes, or images, just test the effectiveness of the testimonial. Design the pieces with a special code within the offer so you know if the piece included the testimonial or not. You can also use a different call tracking number, or require the consumer to bring the entire piece in for the offer to be redeemed, so you can track your results. Your metrics may look something like this:

Direct Mail Campaign: Testimonial Test

Description Results: No Testimonial vs. Testimonial
Number of Pieces Redeemed: 132 without testimonials / 188 with testimonials
Total Resulting Sales: $4,620 without testimonials / $6,580 with testimonials

   This is just an example, but it illustrates the ease of testing different elements within your marketing to determine what works and what doesn't. Sometimes the addition of a single variable has a dramatic impact on the results, while other times the results are subtle. Regardless of the results, the metrics will allow you to continue to improve your approach and campaign design until you have optimized your marketing pieces and created a winning marketing formula. Use this approach to determine if including testimonials will move the needle higher.

Testing Offers: Since we are on the subject, let's cover testing your offers. Just as we tested the effectiveness of the testimonial in the example above, it is important to test your different offers and coupons within your advertising. Many companies and marketing experts are reluctant to feature coupons and special offers in their advertising. They are concerned that coupons will diminish the brand and define their business as a discount player. The business is concerned that they are training the consumer to wait for a deal before they spend money with the business. These concerns are well founded. You need to be very careful in how you execute your offers and coupons. Make them special, unique, and part of a comprehensive effort to build a long-term relationship with your customer. Use them to promote a new product or service. Use them carefully.

   While these concerns are very valid, offers and coupons continue to be the best way to track the results of your advertising. If you elect to use coupons and special offers, it is important to track them to determine which offers work best. Just like the testimonial example above, test your coupons one variable at a time. For example, offer 25% off in 5,000 of the direct mail pieces and $10 off in the other 5,000 pieces. Then track the results. Typically, dollars-off coupons produce better results than percentage off coupons, as the consumer immediately understands that they will be saving $10, while they may not understand how much they will save with 25% off. The $10 off coupon has nearly the same value as a $10 bill in the consumer's mind, especially if it is tied to something they need or want.

Continue to test your offers. Try different percentages, different dollar amounts, feature different products and services. Ask your customer what kind of offers they would be most interested in. Over time, you will refine your offer strategy for the best possible investment returns.

Direct Mail Letters: Direct mail letters, printed on your company letterhead and inserted into a #10 logo envelope, can be extremely effective. There are many marketing books dedicated to direct mail that provide tips for writing and designing your marketing letter campaigns. Here are a few key takeaways:

- **1-Page with Simple Paragraphs:** Keep your business and marketing letters short and to the point, never more than one page. Heavy text and long paragraphs will be quickly filed in the trash can. Use just a few, brief paragraphs to describe your value proposition.
- **Focus on the Customer:** Do not try to tell the recipient everything about your company. Do not dwell on how terrific you are, or discuss your many capabilities in great detail. Rather, focus on their needs and how you can help ***them***. Make your customers the focus of the letter and explain how you can help them reach their goals.
- **PS:** Always include a postscript, or a PS. Most people will skip directly to the PS and read it before they read the rest of the content. Many people will not take the time to read your letter, but they will glance at the PS. The key to this approach is to make your PS summarize your letter content. Some examples follow:

PS: I just learned that Simple, Inc saved $57,000 by installing our new HR software
PS: Next week, I will deliver a free sample of our time-saving Industrial Widget
PS: This free wealth seminar will feature 101 tips for maximizing your net worth

- **Headline:** Headlines can be very effective when added to a sales letter. Consider centering and bolding (or highlighting) a headline above the letter content. Just as people prefer reading the PS over the content within the letter, they will often read the headline before deciding if they want to read the rest of your letter. The headline should focus on the most important needs of your customer. Here are a few examples:

> *You can generate over 1,000 qualified leads*
> *Never Worry About Meeting Payroll Again*
> *Save Money and Time with our Production Software*

Similar techniques can be used in your e-mail solicitations. Before you begin typing, think about the mail that you receive. Consider which letters and e-mails you read and which ones you throw away or delete. Take some time to edit the copy down to a few brief concepts, include a simple value-oriented headline, add a PS that summarizes the content, and make the letter about the customer. These additions to your marketing letters should translate to improved results.

Radio Promotions / Live Remotes / Endorsements: Thinking about advertising on the radio? It can be a very powerful form of advertising for your business. Many consumers form a powerful bond with a radio station and their personalities and they can be very loyal to the companies that support them. Buying radio also allows you to effectively reach your target demographic. If you want to include radio in your marketing mix, use the power of radio to your advantage. As part of your contract, have the radio station(s) include your business in their live remotes, special promotional features, endorsements, and on-air contests. (A quick definition: A *live remote* is when the radio station sets up their broadcasting equipment and their radio personalities at a community event or business and broadcasts "remotely" from that location. Many radio stations have a large following of loyal listeners, and those listeners will often appear at the location of the live remote to experience the event or business that is being promoted by the radio station. Live remotes add excitement to a special event and help to get the word out to the community.)

Ask the radio station to build these sponsorships around your ad campaigns. Radio stations sell air time. Once a moment has passed, it can never be sold again. You can use this to your advantage in negotiating terrific rates for your radio spots, and include the live remotes and special promotions as part of your buy. The radio station personalities can also endorse your product or service, help you produce your spot, and develop metrics so you can track the results.

Promotional Events: Promotions are a fun way to invite your customers to a party. You can meet and greet your customers and use promotional events as a way to launch new products, introduce new services, survey your customers, and encourage your customers to actively participate with your business.

Promotional events can also be expensive, if you are not careful. However, there are many ways to lower your costs. For 10 years, I ran a promotional event on tax night (April 15th) that included several weeks of radio spots, a live 4-hour radio remote, coverage by many of the local television stations and newspapers, bands, free food, prizes and activities for the customers. It was a big event and thousands of people participated. Sound expensive? These annual promotions cost my company less than $1,000…total. True story.

How did we do this? We used volunteer labor. The food was donated by restaurants that wanted to promote their brands at the event. The prizes were donated by the radio station and other companies. The radio time and live remotes were contributed at no charge by the radio station. The bands were eager to get their names into the community and played for free. The television stations and newspapers did not want to miss a good story. And the event was nearly free for my company. We were able to do this because we created the idea. We held the secret ingredients to the promotion. It was our event, we controlled it, and we invited the other companies to participate. We formed a partnership with the radio station that lasted for 10 years. It was a win-win.

You can create a similar event and control it as the title sponsor. These events can take many forms and shapes, like a community golf tournament that supports underprivileged children, a toy drive, a fun run to raise money to cure cancer, a community safety day featuring police and fire personnel and equipment, a parade to celebrate the birthday of your community, or a monster truck rally. It just takes some imagination. These events rarely become a huge success in their first or second year. However, if you stay with them, promote them well, invite lots of people, and feature them in your marketing plan, you will build something very special over time. Notice that many of the ideas provided involve a charity. This is not by coincidence. Giving back to your community is important and should be a key part of your promotional strategy. With careful planning, you can create an event that costs very little money and does much to build awareness for your brand.

Ask Around: Before you sign the advertising contract, contact the other advertisers within the medium or publication and ask a few questions. Find out what they are paying, how long they have advertised with this company, what results they have experienced, would they sign a new contract, what offers or approaches have worked best for them, how they track their results, and where else they advertise. You will learn a great deal from your fellow advertisers. Loaded with this information, you are now ready to negotiate your rates.

Sell the Back Side: Many companies use sell sheets and flyers to promote their businesses. While flyers are relatively inexpensive, there is a way to cut your costs in half, double your distribution, or increase your reach. Form a strategic partnership with a company within your industry or shopping center and place their content on the back of the flyers, while you place your content on the front. Divide the flyers evenly, say 5,000 per business, and then have written objectives for distributing them. The same approach works with door hanger campaigns. If you want to reduce your printing and distribution costs, just add a strategic partner to the back. Just be sure that you have selected a professional, reliable, and ethical strategic partner. Make sure that their content is well designed and well written. You don't want your strategic partner to diminish your brand. Also, selling the back side of flyers and door hangers should be reserved for smaller businesses. This is a terrific tactic for pizza restaurants, bagel shops, dry cleaners, postal stores, ice cream shops, and other retail-oriented businesses. For larger companies, the very act of splitting your flyer design may act to diminish your brand. Be sure that this tactic is consistent with your brand and company image.

Advertising File: Regardless of the size of your company, your marketing department needs to keep complete records of all of your advertising and marketing activities. Copies of the ads, agreements, the resulting metrics for leads and sales, contact information for strategic partnerships, location of native files, and rights to images should all be filed in an organized fashion. You will want to compare your results from year to year and be able to refer back to the actual design and copy that you used. Additionally, if you are ever interested in selling your business, the advertising file will have great value, as it can save the new owner thousands of dollars in trial and error.

Plan Your Advertising Purchases in Advance: You will spend less money if you do your grocery shopping with a list. The same is true with pre-planning your advertising spend within your marketing plan. Before you schedule a meeting with a media company or publication, have your plan in place, with clearly stated objectives and a budget. It is best if you have done your research in advance, by matching their target demographics against your customer profile and speaking with their current advertisers regarding their experiences, what they have paid, and their results. Compare the costs, reach and frequency to other competing stations and publications, so you are in a position of strength in your negotiations. If you are willing to invest in advance planning prior to these meetings, you will negotiate better deals and save critical dollars for your marketing department.

Cooling-Off Period: You may want to consider adding a provision within your advertising agreements for a cooling-off period. This is essentially an out clause that states that you can cancel the contract prior to a certain date. This will provide you with additional time to research the company, verify the effectiveness of the vehicle, plan your advertising campaign, and confirm that this tactic is in line with your marketing plan.

Less is More: Do not try to say everything about your company in a single ad. This will make your advertising look cluttered, unprofessional, and confusing. White space is extremely important in advertising. Make sure that your print ads have plenty of white space and are easy on the eye. Make your copy easy to read and keep all of your headlines at 7 words or less – 3 or less is even better. Within your creative, focus the copy on the benefit(s) that are most important to the consumer. Solve their problem. Do not try to cover everything that you sell. It is too difficult for the consumer to digest everything that you have to offer. Use one simple concept. Feature one compelling benefit. Use one powerful image. Once your ad is finished, see if you can trim the copy by another 40%, while retaining the meaning of your text. You will be surprised how you can edit a thought down to just a few words.

Remove all Obstacles: Never make your customer guess. Do not assume that they know something about your business. Remove all obstacles for doing business with you. Make it easy for them to find your business. If you have a retail business, provide clear, simple directions or a map with identifiable landmarks. If you have a web-based business, feature your web address prominently. If you have a service business, make it easy to see your phone number. Once they find your business, have a plan in place for helping them quickly. Eliminate long forms, long lines, call waiting, and heavy, boring text on your website. Make their experience of doing business with you fast and easy. Control your customers' positive experience by having trained people, working with a proven process, greeting your new customers, and on-boarding them smoothly into your business process. Treat them like honored guests, solve their problems, thank them for visiting, and ask them to please return. You are still marketing to your customers after they have replied to your marketing. Keep the experience alive and positive throughout the entire transaction. Your image is on the line.

The Value of a Customer: Customers are the lifeblood of any business. Without customers, you do not have a business. Be sure to have a comprehensive customer service plan in place to guarantee that every customer has a positive experience with your business.

Add up all of your marketing expenses for the year and divide by the number of new customers. That is your cost to acquire a new customer. So, if you spent $135,000 on marketing last year and it resulted in 1,268 new customers, your cost-per-customer is $106.46. You have invested $106.46 in each customer that contacts you or walks in your door. Make sure that you receive a positive return on your investment by providing your very best customer service to every customer.

A more important figure to consider is your value-per-customer. If you had total sales of $2,585,000 last year with 485 customers, then each one of your customers spent an average of $5,329.89. This is your value-per-customer. In this example, each customer that visits your business has a potential value of $5,329.89. This is a lot of money!

Each customer adds a tremendous amount of value to your business, so it is important to provide every customer with a terrific customer service experience. Additionally, each of these customers has friends, neighbors, and business contacts. In this example, each of these friends has a value of over $5,000 to your business. Ask for introductions to these friends through a formal customer referral program. And be sure to have comprehensive customer service plans in place that cultivate each customer, as they are your most valuable asset. We will discuss customer service in great depth in an upcoming chapter, but it is important to consider the value of your customers and enhance their experience within the context of your advertising.

The ideas and tips provided within this chapter are by no means complete. There are thousands of terrific ideas for lowering your advertising costs and maximizing your results. Hopefully this chapter has provided you with a new perspective for planning your advertising and will save you critical marketing dollars.

In summary, you can save thousands of dollars a year by negotiating your advertising rates. If you apply all of the available discounts and areas of negotiation, you will save a fortune. Some of the areas for saving on your ad spend are mutually exclusive or overlap, while other available discounts can be used in concert. Big savings are available in many places, as summarized by the following example.

Let's say you are interested in placing an advertisement in a major magazine. The accumulated discounts could look something like this:

Example: Half Page, Black & White Print Ad in a Major Magazine

Rate Card Price:	**$14,500.00**

Discount Summary:

Agency Discount @ 15%:	$ 2,175.00
Discount from Rate Card @ 10%:	$ 1,450.00
6X Frequency Discount @ 10%:	$ 1,450.00
Cash-Up Front @ 2%	$ 290.00
Nice Guy Discount @ 5%	$ 1,450.00
Total Savings:	**$ 6,185.00**

Total Cost Per Ad:	**$ 7,685.00**

This is a significant discount. Over 6 issues, the savings on this ad will be $37,100.

However, this is not all that has been negotiated. In addition to price reductions, extras have been added to the contract. The list follows:

Free Graphic Design Added	$ 350.00
4-Color Included at No Cost	$ 1,500.00
Ad Size Increased to ¾ Page	$ 1,200.00
Feature Article:	$ 850.00
Total Value of Extras:	**$ 3,900.00**

As a result of these negotiations, we are receiving a single ad valued at $18,400, for only $7,685. This is an incredible discount. The total savings for the 6X campaign is over $64,000. However, we are not done yet.

We can now apply co-op dollars from a key supplier for half of the cost of the ad. If the cost of our ad is $7,685, the co-op dollars contributed will be $ 3,842.50. The addition of co-op dollars boosts the total savings on this campaign from $64,000 to over $87,000!

In summary, we are receiving an advertisement worth $18,400 for only $3,842.50!

This is just an example, and not all of these discounts will be available with every buy. Market forces will have an impact on the cost of advertising. When your industry is hot, these rates will go up and negotiating will be difficult. However, when the market is soft, greater discounts may be available. The point of the exercise is to demonstrate the available savings. Realizing the full value of these potential savings is up to you and your negotiating skills.

We will now apply the same money-saving tips and ideas to other critical aspects of your marketing plan, including your marketing collateral and direct mail campaigns.

CHAPTER 10:
MARKETING COLLATERAL

Marketing encompasses the tangible, as well. The design and function of your marketing collateral pieces are critical to carrying your brand forward, executing your strategy, and connecting with your target customer. These critical pieces must be consistent with the brand you present in your messaging, on your website, in your broadcast media, and within your mission statement. They are the pieces that help you close business, sustain relationships, convey your message, and prove your convictions. They are important fixtures of your formula marketing.

One of my clients for many years has been a large commercial printing company in Southern California. Over the years, they have taught me a great deal about printing and marketing collateral. They specialize in printing high-quality marketing collateral for some of the largest companies in the region. They have a tagline that captures the essence of marketing collateral, "Your Vision on Paper". That states it precisely.

Marketing collateral is more than brochures and flyers. In fact, it is difficult to capture everything in a single list, but here are some of the most common pieces:

- Business Cards
- Letterhead
- Envelopes
- Brochures
- Presentation Folders
- Note Cards
- Invitations
- Sell Sheets
- Direct Mail Pieces
- Newsletters

- Invoices
- Presentation Materials
- Forms
- Packaging
- Inserts
- Work Books & Binders
- Instruction Sheets
- Manuals
- Calendars
- Thank You Cards
- Membership Cards
- Coupon Books
- POP Displays
- Posters
- Shelf Signs
- Table Tents

And the list goes on.

Printing can be extremely expensive, so you want to get the most out of your marketing dollars as you create your collateral. You also want to make sure that you always project the right image with your marketing collateral. It takes thousands and thousands of dollars to build your brand, and you can diminish it overnight with a poorly designed, low quality collateral piece. The following tips should help you get the most from your marketing collateral.

Longer Print Runs Produce The Best Unit Price: In traditional offset printing, the more you print of a given item, the lower the unit price. The price to print 5,000 sell sheets is only a little higher than the cost to print 1,000. The price to print 100,000 brochures is marginally higher than printing 50,000. Once the pre-press work is complete, the plates are made, and the printing press is set-up, a good portion of the cost of the print order has been allocated. The paper stock and labor increase with a longer print run, but only nominally. If you can use the additional brochures within other marketing tactics, you might as well keep the press running. If you only need a certain number of pieces to distribute to your sales force, mail to your customer base, or hand out at your trade shows, consider other uses for the same piece.

It is important to design the additional uses into the piece during the creative stage of collateral development. Ask your creative team questions like: Can your main marketing brochure double as a direct mail piece? Can we use these sell sheets as newspaper inserts or trade show bag stuffers? Can our newsletter be inserted into our billing statements or invoices? Can we display these posters on the local college campuses and at sports venues? Can our POP displays be used as table tents? Can our note cards be used as invitations and thank-you cards, too? Consolidating your collateral buys will help to use your marketing dollars more effectively, while conveying a concise and streamlined brand statement.

Before you authorize a long print-run, be sure your marketing pieces will not become quickly obsolete. If possible, avoid including pricing information, dates, seasons, or exact specifications on your longer print run pieces. Obsolete collateral material is extremely wasteful and expensive.

Personalized Collateral: At the other end of the spectrum, digital printing technology has made extremely short print runs cost effective. It is now possible to print a single brochure, customized for a single customer. You can print multiple versions of pieces to focus on different industries, all within a single print run. You are able to print your customer's names, addresses, graphics and text on your collateral piece that appeals directly to their demographic. So long as the printed pieces are the same size (like a 9X6 postcard) you can print thousands of completely different artwork versions in a single print run.

The advantages of digital printing are clear. While it often carries a higher per unit price, digital printing eliminates obsolescence, reduces waste, and eliminates the need for plates and costly set-up. Digital printing is faster, too. With delivery dates of hours instead of days, you have a great deal more freedom in your production schedules.

It has been proven that a direct mail piece or brochure that is customized for your target customer will typically double your response rates. If your static, generic direct mail pieces are currently yielding a 1% return, personalizing that same piece and including messages relevant to your customer, including their name and targeting their needs and wants, will boost the rate of return to 2% or higher. This is a big deal. While the cost may be higher, your final results will produce greater sales and higher profits.

Special Coatings: It is critical to add a special coating, either UV or aqueous, to your direct mail pieces. The USPS systems are punishing to direct mail and your image will be quickly smeared or tarnished. Adding a special coating will protect your graphics and ensure that a more professional looking piece is delivered to your customer. Coatings are relatively inexpensive, so it is a good idea to coat everything that you print, if appropriate. High gloss coatings can support a high-quality, luxurious image, while a textured coating will appeal to the senses. Coatings come in different types and finishes; ask around for samples and begin to add them to your collateral. It is often possible to negotiate your printing costs, and asking for discounts on your coatings is a request many printers will accommodate.

Paper Selections: There are thousands of grades, finishes and thicknesses of paper. Choose your paper carefully and be consistent with its use. Be sure to use the same papers across all of your collateral pieces. Ask your printer for samples, swatch books, and suggestions.

Consistent Branding: Be sure to have a professional design your collateral pieces to work together. Make sure your colors, logos and images are consistent across all of your collateral pieces. Use the same logo, placement and paper stock on your letterhead, envelopes and business cards. Make sure your direct mail pieces match your newsletters and presentation materials. Design your invoices, packing slips, forms and inserts to carry your brand message. Carefully select your corporate colors and call them out in your artwork and brand standards. Work with a single, high-quality commercial printer to secure the best price and maintain your brand standards across all pieces. Think of your printer as your strategic partner. He can do much to help you execute your tactics and strategies.

Testimonials: Include testimonials in your collateral pieces. They will strengthen your messaging, add conviction to your marketing claims, and allow your customers to do some preliminary due diligence. As discussed in an earlier chapter, including testimonials will also boost the results of your direct mail campaigns.

Carefully consider all of your collateral pieces in advance of printing them. Map out a strategy that enhances your brand, supports your marketing calendar, and consistently executes your core marketing matrix. When your collateral is created in concert with your marketing formula, it will translate directly to your bottom line.

CHAPTER 11:
MARKETING ON THE INTERNET

I want to be quick to state that I am not an expert in Internet marketing. I say this even though I have done a great deal of Internet marketing, routinely build and support on-line marketing support sites for my corporate clients, and I own a social media company that is focused on developing content for corporations via blogs, e-PR, websites, FaceBook, Twitter, LinkedIn and other social networking sites. With these credentials, I am far from an expert on Internet marketing. The fact is, the Internet moves so fast and changes so quickly, that it is very difficult to lead the trends. However, following marketing trends on the Internet can pay huge dividends for your business.

Developing an Internet strategy is critical to your marketing plan. The Internet is how much of America shops. For the first time in history, your retail business in Ames, Iowa can serve the globe through an online store front. This is truly amazing. Your customers can now visit your business from all around the world. This gives you access to a host of new customers and revenue streams. To pass on these opportunities is more than short-sighted, it is madness.

The approach you take to implement your Internet marketing tactics should be no different than the approach used for traditional marketing. You need to develop a Situational Analysis, define your Objectives, create your Strategies, select your Tactics and evaluate your results through your Assessment. The classic 5 steps of your marketing plan must include the Internet activities needed to build your brand, support your clients and drive sales into your organization.

The Internet has so many facets and opportunities that I will not try to cover them all in a single chapter. There are whole books devoted to Internet marketing and you should certainly consider reading a few of them if this topic is elusive to you. However, with the short time we have together, we will focus on the top elements of Internet marketing.

Websites: Business websites are changing. They used to be online marketing brochures, with introductory and important information about a company. Websites contained information about the product line, the services available, and provided information about the company and the key employees. Websites included the company mission statement, testimonials, and directions to locate the business.

Today's websites are more interactive. They allow you to connect directly to your customers and get their feedback immediately on what they think of your products and services. The same customer communicates with one another and offer ideas to enhance company products. Website's now offer on-line presentations that guide prospective consumers through the buying process, or explain the core value proposition. Today's websites offer dynamic customer surveys, retail store fronts with sophisticated shopping carts, and easy-to-use and secure payment systems. With programs like Google Analytics, you can see who visits your website, how often they visit, which pages they toured, and what they clicked on. You can also determine with some accuracy who these people are, where they live, and what they like to buy.

Websites are personalized now, too. With sophisticated PURL (Personal URL) programs via direct mail and e-blasts, you can invite your target clients to visit a website that is designed just for them, with their name designed into the site, and an emphasis on the products and services that they are most likely interested in. You can install alerts on your website to send you a text or e-mail when a target client is visiting your site. You can call them immediately and say, "I see you are on our website right now, can I answer any questions for you?" Pretty amazing!

Websites can change with each visit, where the introduction Flash video can be disabled after the second visit, where the home page can change rapidly. Website traffic is increasing, too. Faster and more precise search engines are guiding more sophisticated buyers to high-touch, high-tech experiences online.

The Internet is not always your friend. Your customers can now search the Internet for your same products and services at better prices, with more features, and better service. Services like Yelp.com can destroy the reputation of an established restaurant overnight. Your entire staff can be subject to free, intensive background searches. And your competition can drill into your code and develop strategies to rank higher than you on the popular search engines.

With promise comes peril, and you simply need to develop an Internet marketing strategy that works for your business. Develop a website that is easy to find via Google and other search engines. Build your website in a fashion that aligns with the terrain of the Internet, like html, rather than a program like Flash, so it is easier for the search engines to locate your content. Design your website as a professional and interactive marketing brochure for your business. Add features that allow you to connect with your customers. Give them ownership of your website and provide on-line presentations, videos, and links to other sites that will interest them. Include an SEO strategy that makes your website easy to find and lands you on the first page of Google and other search engines, especially if most of your customers are buying from you via the Internet. Carefully select and incorporate your key words, link to hundreds of other sites, and actively post your e-PR to news websites around the web.

Include stand alone revenue streams that allow your customers to buy from you online. Provide tools that allow your customers to calculate their savings, create their design, build their own quote, design their prototype, and order their next project.

Search your competitor's websites and see what they have to offer. Study their approaches. Determine how they rank on the search engine pages. Are they linked to other businesses? Do your suppliers support their website? Can you beat them at their own game? Or do you work with them? Does it make sense to form an association with your competitors and link together, just as car dealerships cluster their lots to make it easier for the consumer to shop?

Consider how your website supports your brand. Spend some time thinking about how your website helps you sell your products. Visit your website like a customer and evaluate the experience. Run diagnostics on your website to reveal the weaknesses for competitive search engine rankings. Ask your customers to help you design your website and improve it as a tool for their use.

Your clients will evaluate if you are a serious player by the design and composition of your website. If nothing else, be sure that your website presents a professional and up-to-date image of your company. Websites are changing quickly. And you can respond by adapting your website to thrive on the new Internet. You are, as they say, just a few clicks away.

SEO: Search Engine Optimization, or SEO, is critical for many businesses. Landing the number one ranking on a key word search, or hitting high on the front page of searches within your industry is a new and highly competitive game on the Internet. Companies are spending thousands and thousands of dollars on SEO strategies to boost their search rankings. Expert SEO companies are sprouting up across the world, offering agency-like services at both reasonable and outrageous prices. Imagine the pressure on an SEO company to appear as the number one ranked SEO business on Google! If they are really the best, they should have the highest ranking.

SEO is important. However, is it the best investment for your business? At some level, you want to build your website with all of the features necessary to provide you with a good search engine ranking. You may decide one day that you need to improve your search engine ranking and redesigning your website to rank higher can be very expensive. So design the features (like key words and links) that control your rank into the foundation of your website.

Should SEO command the majority of your budget? "Yes" answers this question if your customers find you exclusively on the Internet and you are in a highly competitive category. However, for most businesses, SEO should be one of several tactics within their marketing portfolio. Devote a portion of your budget to SEO-related tactics, but continue to build your brand through a well balanced marketing matrix. Remember to test your SEO expenditures and calculate your ROI through each activity. If SEO is driving revenue, increasing sales, and boosting profits, then continue. However, if SEO is merely boosting traffic to your website but not impacting your bottom line, you should test changes to your website to improve your results, or minimize your SEO commitments.

Developing metrics for your SEO activities is fairly easy. You should know which customers are finding you via native searches, versus those customers that are finding you via paid online advertising. You should have an accurate picture of the leads, proposals, sales, and referrals that were generated via search engines. Study these metrics to determine how best to allocate your marketing budget going forward.

E-Campaigns: More than a series of e-mails to your database, e-blast campaigns are a very cost-effective way to connect with your customers. E-blasts can operate like a personalized, targeted direct mail campaign, with links to PURLS, websites, and online demonstrations. E-campaigns can include all of the data analytics and tracking devices that will provide reports on who opened the e-mail, who clicked through, and what they did once they landed on your website.

Without the cost of printing and postage, e-blasts are extremely cost effective. It is easy to set-up a series of e-blast templates that allow you to customize your creative, upload your database and send your campaign out on a schedule. You can coordinate your e-blasts with other marketing tactics, like direct mail, direct sales, special events, and promotional items, to create a comprehensive direct marketing campaign. If you are not currently using e-campaigns in your marketing plan, consider adding them to your arsenal.

The key to an effective e-mail campaign is gathering the e-mail addresses from your customers. Begin doing this in your surveys, on your website forms, and through your traditional marketing contacts. Build a database of customer e-mail addresses and then leverage it over time on your e-campaigns. However, you must be very careful to build your e-mail database with the approval of your customers. As you gather their e-mail addresses, be sure to let them know that you plan to send special offers, newsletters, and other communications via e-mail. Allow your clients to opt-in to these campaigns, rather than spam them without their permission. You want to build a positive relationship with your customers, not overwhelm them with a tsunami of e-mails.

E-PR: One of my clients recently announced a new strategic partnership. We developed a marketing campaign to announce it to their customers. As part of the launch, we developed a press release and distributed it throughout the Internet through an e-PR newswire. Within minutes, the press release was converted into an article on over 2.5 million news websites. This is amazing! I used to work for hours to place my PR with a few local newspapers, but now, with the Internet, you can reach millions of publications in seconds. Internet newswires are not expensive and they serve as a great way to get the word out quickly. Links to hundreds of news websites will dramatically boost your SEO rankings and will allow consumers to find you more easily on the web.

YouTube: Consider developing a campaign that includes a video or series of videos on YouTube. Link your Internet PR to these videos to drive more traffic to them. Feature your YouTube videos on your website and add links to the videos within each outbound e-mail.

The equipment to create your own videos is inexpensive and very accessible. You do not need to hire an expensive production company, but be sure to enhance your brand with your videos, rather than producing a video that could diminish your brand. If you have a polished image and have invested millions to establish your brand, hiring a professional production firm could be the best way to go.

YouTube is hot at time of the writing of this book. Another site or approach may quickly overtake YouTube as the premier video and marketing resource. The key is to follow the Internet trends and continue to test and refine your Internet strategy.

Online Advertising: There are a great many places to advertise on the Internet. There are directories, like Franchise Gator and Service Magic, and other high-traffic industry-specific sites that allow banner advertising. Pop-up ads can be linked to visits on like-minded sites and can connect directly to your website or landing pages. You can advertise on Google by paying for a sponsored link that appears with the top rankings on the first page. You can advertise with popular online publications, like USAToday, MSNBC, and the Wall Street Journal. While the mediums are different, the principles are the same. Continue to test and refine your advertising, negotiate your rates, track and assess your results, and be sure to align your Internet advertising strategy with your core strategies.

Social Media: Social networking is currently very popular on the Internet and this is not likely to change. Corporations are posting their own blogs on Wordpress.com, maintaining FaceBook accounts, tweeting special offers via Twitter, and building networks on LinkedIn. They are linking their social media together with programs like Tweet Deck, so each post updates the others. Fans are following their favorite companies and getting the inside track on special offers, new menu items, and limited edition specials.

I was recently speaking with a restaurant chain about their social networking strategy. They tweeted a special food offer via Twitter one evening and long lines formed around each location by the next day. Powerful!

Social media is inexpensive, builds loyalty within your core demographic, and grows quickly and organically. It will also boost your SEO rankings and provide fresh new content to your website.

Social media opens the door to your customers to share their experiences with your business, both good and bad. You can interact with them directly, listen to their ideas, promote your success, address their concerns and defend your actions. It is a brave new world online and it is time to get social.

There is a great deal more to talk about concerning Internet marketing. The most exciting things have not yet been developed, but they are just around the corner. Our phones and PDAs are turning into personal shoppers, directing us to the best deals and the new hot spots. Smarter computers, faster processors, lower prices, and burgeoning usage are all contributing to the creation of the greatest marketplace in the history of the world. Fortunes are being created online and you need to set your strategy, dive in, and begin thriving there. It's a bold new world and not for the faint of heart. Yet launching into brave new territory, taking risks, trying new approaches, and mastering a changing marketplace will always be at the heart of business.

CHAPTER 12:
TRADESHOW MARKETING

Within certain industries, commerce begins at the tradeshow. New products are launched, contracts are signed, key decision makers walk the aisles, and important meetings are held in booths, hallways, and nearby hotel suites. When executed well, a company can accomplish more at an industry tradeshow than in 6 months of direct sales and marketing. Some companies embrace the tradeshow and maximize their potential, accelerating their pipeline development and turning their corporate objectives into tangible sales. However, for every company that excels at tradeshow execution, there are dozens more that just show up, set up a booth and hope for the best. There is a distinct difference between the two approaches. In this chapter, we will focus on getting the most from your tradeshow marketing.

Location, Location, Location: Think of the tradeshow as a small city, or a shopping mall. There are good locations and very poor locations. Location is EVERYTHING at a tradeshow. The location of your booth sends an immediate message about the identity of your company within the industry. You can tell right away if a company is an industry leader, or a newcomer; well financed, or on a shoe-string budget. The size of the booth is not important, it is the location that matters.

The tradeshow sites are usually reserved well in advance, with the best spots given to the companies that have been at the show for many years, or spend the most money on the multi-space booths. If you are a newcomer to a tradeshow, you will often be relegated to the second or third ballroom down the hallway, or the *basement* (gasp!).

Do not accept these locations. Everyone visits the main hall. You need to negotiate your way into the main hall. The main hall is where the action is, where the announcements take place, where the big players are, and where the FOOD and the BAR are located. Do whatever it takes to get into the main hall. And once in the main hall, work hard to get near the *entrance*, on the *main aisle*, or near the *food and drinks*.

As you negotiate your spot with the tradeshow host company, offer to spend more money to secure your location in the main hall, or on the main aisle. If there is a wait list, offer to pay more money to move up the list. Offer to sponsor a prize for their drawing, host dessert for the conference, advertise in the program, or provide tradeshow bags for the attendees. Meet with the tradeshow host company representative in person, if possible. Sit down with him and work-out a multi-year deal that secures a better site. Be willing to be flexible on your booth configuration or accept a smaller booth size, but be sure you secure the best possible location at the tradeshow. It is critical to your success at the show.

Think about it. The key decision makers, the CEOs, the people with money to invest, the new project PhDs, they are all too busy to visit every booth in every ballroom. They carve sufficient time out of their schedules to visit the main hall for a few hours. You need to be in the main hall and in a great location within the main hall. That is where the action is. A good location at an important tradeshow will establish your business for years to come. Invest in the best location and then execute well.

Over-Staff: I am always amazed that companies spend thousands of dollars to appear at a tradeshow, but then they fail to adequately staff their booth. Booths are often left vacant during lunch, restroom breaks or important meetings. Every second that a booth is vacant, potential profits are lost. The director of international purchasing, Mr. Murakami, may stop by your booth, see no one is there and visit your competitor instead. Ouch! Millions were just lost. Mrs. Swanson just re-financed her home, she has cash to spend on a project, and wants the product you are selling. If you are not there to answer her questions and book an at-home consultation, the purchase will be made through someone else.

Thinly staffed booths are just as bad for business. Business customers often travel in groups at tradeshows. You need adequate staff to assign a person to every visitor. No one wants to listen to someone else asking questions. No one wants to wait more than a minute to talk to someone in a tradeshow booth.

Most tradeshow booths are staffed with one or two people. They sit in their chairs and wait for the world to come to them. Visiting a booth of "aisle watchers" is like going to a boring party. Rather, you need to throw a party in your booth. Fill it with fun people, who are dressed professionally, smiling and happy. Invite the friendly, outgoing people from your office. They do not have to be in sales, marketing or engineering. Bring in people from *all* departments. They can discuss their functions with the potential customers. Trust me. The customer will be impressed when the whole team is there. They will enjoy speaking with your engineers, your installation team, your receptionist, training staff, your HR department, top brass and CEO. If these people are not available, bring your family, friends and strategic partners. Fill your booth with young, attractive fun people. Make a scene and stand out from the other *boring* tradeshow booths.

Fill the booth with your people; 10 or 20 people at a tradeshow is not too many. Eight to ten people can staff the booth, while the others walk the floors. Ideally, they are all wearing logo polo or dress shirts so the whole assembly will see your branding as they wander and mingle. They will see you at the tradeshow in full force. You now have sufficient staff to attend the meetings and white paper presentations, talk to other vendors and discuss strategic partnerships, attend the cocktail parties, and make new friends. If it is a big tradeshow, do not hold back on bringing your people. Your whole company can learn more about your business at a tradeshow then in 2 years in their cubicles. They can gather critical intelligence on your competition, determine their pricing strategy, and hire key people away from other companies. Tradeshows are industry events, so create an event in your booth by filling it with your staff.

Make It Fun to Visit Your Booth: Boring booths are not visited at a tradeshow. Everyone goes to where the fun is. The talk of the tradeshow is usually, "How did you do at Widget's putting competition?" or "I hit the bulls eye at the Alliance booth and just won this prize. You gotta give it a try!"

People like to have fun. The tradeshow gets them out of the office and they are ready to unwind. They will not unwind talking about your products or services. Loosen them up a little with a fun computer game, trivia contest, Nerf dart guns, or some soft-serve ice cream. Make the games short, so the line moves quickly. Make them easy, so the novice can win. Have a team there to cheer when someone wins. The whole tradeshow will hear the cheers and wonder what is happening at your booth.

Consider hosting a drawing with an assortment of prizes. Work with the tradeshow host company to add your drawing to the agenda and offer to let them handle the announcements. Be sure to have the drawing in front of your booth and get full credit for the prizes by printing-up special raffle tickets with your corporate branding.

Assign your friendliest people to be greeters that stand in the aisle and welcome new customers to your booth. Don't just let people wander by, smiling and reading your posters, greet them in the aisle and invite them to have some candy, try your game, or enter your drawing for a big screen TV. This tactic works extremely well and will keep your booth filled with people, which will draw more people.

Be the party host at the tradeshow. This is not the time to be shy, reserved, or overly professional. Connect with your customers over a good dose of fun.

Food & Promotional Items: Tradeshows are famous for candy, food, and promotional items. These are great tools for connecting with your customers.

The promotional products business has expanded exponentially to create thousands of new, clever items to brand with your corporate logo. There are thousands of designs for pens, letter openers and mouse pads. If your company is in the financial services industry, millions of coin banks and calculators are available. If you are in the construction trades, measuring tapes, levels, and all-in-one tools are available at all price points. There are promotional products designed for every industry.

A quick Internet search will help you find unique items that will align with your brand. For example, there is a paper manufacturing company that uses a robot within their branding. At commercial printing tradeshows, they pass out robot shaped stress balls. These promotional items literally fly out of their booths. My kids love them and always ask me to bring home new robots from the show. This paper company's logo has been prominently displayed in my home for several years now. Many tradeshow attendees have children, so try to find an item that can go home to the kids, or sit on a C-level desk.

Many tradeshow booths offer candy, so provide the best of show from your company. A quick visit to Walmart or Target will load up a candy dish inexpensively. Keep it full of everyone's favorite candies, like M&Ms, Hershey's candy bars, and mini Crunch bars. Leave the cheesy hard candies to your competition and serve up the good stuff at your booth. Use a giant bowl and keep it filled to overflowing.

You can serve other kinds of food, too. Consider placing an old-fashioned popcorn maker in your booth and serve up bags printed with your logo. It will make your corporate image POP! Offer bottles of water, again tagged with your logo on the label. I have already mentioned mini soft-serve ice cream – this is a cool addition to any booth. Or become a hero and set up a coffee bar within your booth each morning, which will be sure to open some eyes.

The key is to be different and stand apart from the other booths. Make it fun for people to visit you and establish your brand as an innovative leader that is exciting to do business with. Your tradeshow booth should be a direct reflection of your company.

Sponsorships and Ads: Most industry trade shows will publish programs or show guides. Find out what the rates are to advertise in these publications. Negotiate well, just as we discussed in previous chapters. Use your flyers and postcards from other marketing activities and ask to insert them into the event publication. Add a label with your booth location, so the attendees can find you easily.

Many shows allow sponsorships of their event banners, floor signs, and bags. Sponsorships are often available for the cocktail parties, golf tournaments, food service, special events, and after-parties. Negotiate favorable terms as part of your entire trade show booth package. These events can quickly establish your company as a leader within your industry.

Get the most out of your trade show sponsorships. Park your wrapped vehicles in the main hall, or just outside the convention center. Fill the neighboring hotels and restaurants with your flyers, banners, and promotional items. You can also set up mini-preview booths in these locations, and pass out invitations to your booth, event programs and directions. Set up a newspaper stand and give away free newspapers wrapped with your logo and inserted with your marketing flyers. Or print your own daily newspaper, with interesting information about the show, the golf tournament, or the cocktail party. Add lots of photos of people having fun and be sure to feature your company in a few of the articles. These newspapers can be passed out at the show, slid under the hotel room doors by the staff, or added to the convention bags.

I know of a small, technology company that could not compete with the industry leaders within a tradeshow, so they rented a fleet of Vespas, tagged them temporarily with their logos and zipped them around the event and the surrounding venues. They sponsored the city buses, booked ads on the bus benches in front of the convention center, and parked their corporate vehicles in the most prominent parking spaces. While they did not have the largest presence within the show, they dominated the streets around the show.

Hosting the After-Party: Sponsoring the event cocktail parties can be extremely expensive. As a lower-cost alternative, host a smaller "invitation-only" after party, immediately following the "official" cocktails. You can provide a light, creative dinner, themed drinks, and a more relaxed setting. Drawings, prizes, and product demos can anchor your event. Keep the evening short and fun, these people are most likely tired, or eager to tour the city.

Inviting Customers to Visit Your Booth: Before every tradeshow, it is important to invite your current and prospective clients to visit your booth at the event. Send out a personal invitation, using your database and digital printing technology, that offers each client a free gift, chance to win, demonstration of new technology, or special pricing opportunities. The invitations can be either very simple or very sophisticated. Be sure to leverage the abilities of digital printing to include the recipient's name, company, and contact information. Incorporate images that are aligned with their industry and will appeal to their needs and desired benefits. The more personalized the invitation, the more powerful the impact. Provide a map and booth number on the invitation so they can find you easily.

For your top prospects and clients, offer to pay for their registration, enclose a guest pass, or cover the cost of their parking. Add an element to the invitation that encourages them to bring it with them to the show, something like "Redeem this Invitation at our Booth for a Chance to Win a Dinner for Two at the Restaurant of Your Choice". Retain the redeemed invitations for the drawing and then calculate your metrics to determine the results from the invitations.

Setting Advance Meetings: Use the opportunity of being in the same city, or at the same conference, to set up meetings and presentations with your top clients and prospects. Book a nearby hotel room, meet them at a restaurant, or add a conference room to your booth space. You can accomplish a great deal of business at a tradeshow, but it requires advance planning. This is another reason to bring the whole team to your tradeshows, so you can adequately cover the booth, key meetings, mingle responsibilities, cocktail parties, and the golf tournament. You can meet with your strategic partners, cut deals with your top vendors, and write a lot of business at a tradeshow.

Immediate Response to Visitors: During the show, have a mechanism in place to thank your visitors for visiting your booth. Have a simple online Thank-You card template developed that allows you, with a few keystrokes, to upload the database of attendees, or type their names into a personalized Thank-You card. Once you send the order to the digital press, or e-mail it back to your office, your supplier or other staff members can mail out the Thank-You card immediately, so it arrives on your customer's desk the next day, or by the time they return to their office a few days later. You could also send a business Thank-You letter, and enclose a personalized brochure with more information or specification on the product or service they were most interested in.

Your customers will be very impressed with your immediate follow-up. Most sales professionals take several days or weeks to thank the people that visited their tradeshow booth. By the time the customer receives their piece, they will struggle to remember their interest or the specific conversation. By contrast, you will look highly efficient, professional and organized, which sends a very positive message to your customer. They are more likely to remember you and your company, which will greatly improve your opportunity to do business. Be sure to have a plan within the Thank-You card, offering to follow up with a phone call, visit their office or home for a free estimate, or invite them for a tour of your facility. This level of planning will help you establish a better pipeline of prospects and close more business.

Develop a Consistent Follow-Up Plan until the Next Show: Continue to follow up with the prospective customers that visited you at the tradeshow. Just because you did not hear from them immediately does not mean they were not interested in your company. They may be waiting for the new fiscal year to allocate the capital expense for your product, or saving money for their home remodeling project. These customers are also a great source of referrals. Continue to keep in touch with these important decision-makers. You have paid a great deal of money for each of these leads; stay in contact with them. Over time, they may do business with you.

Map out a calendar of follow-up materials that keep these prospects in the loop, while not barraging them with junk mail. Send them product updates, recent newsletters, money-saving tips, and an invitation to the next tradeshow or event. Add these important people to your Christmas card list or e-campaigns. Offer a special seminar, a whitepaper presentation, product demonstration, or facility tour. If you have hundreds of leads, consider hosting an Open House at your office or facility. The key is to keep in touch with these important people. A thorough, long-term approach will yield many future sales and provide a greater return on your tradeshow investment.

Book Next Year Now: While you are at the tradeshow, make arrangements to book your tradeshow booth for the next year. You will be able to lock in this year's prices, reserve the best possible location, and negotiate directly with the show host. You may have noticed some special sponsorships or events that other companies were involved with at the show and you can ask to be included in these for the next year. The show host wants to book you in advance and they often offer special show discounts that will save you a great deal of money for making an advance commitment.

Strategic Partners: Tradeshows are filled with strategic partners, as well. Capitalize on the tradeshow and meet with as many of these companies as possible. All of these companies are actively marketing their brands, or they would not be at the show. Meet with them to determine how you can work together, share leads, co-sponsor future events, secure co-op dollars, formalize agreements, and team up on other marketing programs. You can stretch your marketing dollars dramatically by joining forces with the non-competing firms within your industry.

In summary, tradeshows operate as microcosms of your business plan. You have a product launch, a retail location, a marketplace filled with prospects and customers, many competitors, and hundreds of opportunities. Take advantage of these factors by writing a mini-marketing plan for each tradeshow. Write your Situational Analysis, Objectives, Strategies, Tactics, and Assessment. Develop metrics for each step of the process and each marketing tactic that you deploy. Establish your marketing matrix of the core tactics that will ensure success and a terrific ROI from the event. Cover all of the possibilities with advance invitations, organizing your staff, staging an exciting booth presentation, booking on-site meetings, sending immediate Thank-You's, planning thorough follow-up, and developing a long-term client retention strategy. With a professional marketing formula in place for every tradeshow event, your business will be a force in the industry.

CHAPTER 13:
PUBLIC RELATIONS

There is no reason to be intimidated by public relations. However, many companies do not add public relations to their marketing plan because they think they need an agency or PR experience to be successful.

The truth is, PR tactics are fairly straightforward and easy to execute. The steps within a public relations campaign are not too different from other marketing tactics. However, I believe the key reason marketing departments are reluctant to invest in their own in-house PR efforts is that the results can be elusive. Articles in newspapers and television coverage do not often directly translate to lead generation or direct sales.

I recently had lunch with the top public relations executive for a large, national company. He shared the same frustrations with me. He stated that it was very difficult to prove his worth to the company, because he lacked the tangible results to do so. Over pasta, we developed a series of strategies and tactics that would make it possible for him to create meaningful metrics for his public relations efforts. The objective was to tie his PR successes directly to leads and sales. Within the chapter, we will discuss some ideas for implementing public relations metrics within your formula marketing.

I find that companies generally fall into three groups when it comes to public relations:
(1) They have a PR budget and an agency that handles their PR for them.
(2) They have no budget for PR, so they don't do any PR at all.
(3) They have no budget for PR, but they adeptly handle their own PR.

Do you fall into one of these groups? If so, which one?

My goal is to encourage those of you in Group 2 to join the companies having success with their own PR efforts in Group 3. I also hope to provide a few fresh ideas for the folks in Group 1 and Group 3. There are many terrific books dedicated to PR and I strongly suggest that you find and study the best of them. This book will provide an overview only. However, I hope to encourage you to take the next steps in adding PR as a core element within your marketing matrix.

Find the Story Angle: Good public relations is not just about your company. Editors, writers and news agencies are not interested in the day-to-day operations of your business. They also know that their readers are not directly interested in your business milestones. They want a story. They are looking for an interesting angle. They want to inspire and edify their readership.

When you develop your in-house press, be sure to deliver the *goods* to the editors, writers, and news agencies: story, angle, inspiration, and edification (or education). Without these elements, you will rarely see your business featured in local or national newspapers, and you will rarely be covered by television, Internet or other broadcast media.

So what makes a story? The following list provides a few ideas for story angles that often find their way into print:

- Grand Opening
- Launch of New Business
- Minority Business Ownership Becomes Successful
- Local Boy or Girl Becomes Successful
- Stories with a Seasonal Angle like Christmas, Tax Season, and Mother's Day
- Business Owner Overcomes Hardship to Become Successful
- Creative Idea Becomes a Successful Business
- Business Makes Breakthrough Discovery
- Business Initiates or Reacts to Market-Changing Events
- Current Market Trends Exhibited within a Business
- Business Reacts with Success to Current Market Trends
- Announcing New Product Launch
- Announcing Strategic Partnerships
- Announcing New Key Executive with Interesting Background
- Bad News About the Business
- Controversy or Intrigue About the Business
- Business Receives Local or National Award
- Business Receives Special Grants
- Business Stands for Something (giving to public cause, charity, etc…)
- Business Makes Large Donation
- Business Hosts A Community Event
- Business Does Something Unexpected, Inventive, or Humorous

This is not a complete list, but it gives you some insight into the angles that many editors are looking for. The key with any public relations effort or press release is not to position the content as a commercial for your company. The editor will suggest that you contact the advertising sales department for any self-serving initiative that you attempt to promote. Rather, they are looking for a story.

Writing a Press Release: When you write your press release, be sure to do so in a fashion that makes the editor's job as easy as possible. All of the relevant details, the Who, What, Where, Why, When, and How, should be covered succinctly within the first paragraph.

When possible, keep your press release to a single page. The next paragraph should tell the story through someone's eyes, within the context of a quote from a key individual that is directly involved with the story, typically a customer, top executive, or the CEO. Make the quote as compelling as possible, and use it as a device to fill in the details of the story quickly. A sample press release follows:

Sample Press Release Below

David Wilkey

Local Furniture Maker Switches Production Facility to Wind Power

Albuquerque, NM. (May 15): Classic Comfort, an Albuquerque-based manufacturer of furniture and home accessories, has announced the addition of wind power to their "Green House" environmental strategy. By purchasing 2,100 annual Megawatt-hours of Renewable Energy Credits (RECs) to offset 100% of the energy used by the Classic Comfort production facilities and offices, Classic Comfort has taken another important step in conserving the Earth's natural resources. This annual commitment has the equivalent environmental benefit of planting 953 acres of trees or taking 718 cars off local roads.

"Our wind power initiative is closely aligned with our company strategy to source and develop new and improved options that support the environment within our business operations," stated Eugene Maxwell, president of Classic Comfort. "Our Green House environmental program is a company-wide initiative to incorporate energy-saving efforts that provide the greatest possible benefits for our environment, our community and the homes of our customers."

"We knew our customers wanted to purchase green products for their homes. So we decided to provide them with furnishing options that they could be proud of. Many of our first steps to be environmentally friendly were just common sense," reports Mark Simmons, marketing manager at Classic Comfort. "These early steps have evolved into a comprehensive program to recycle everything we use in production, distribution, and marketing. We only purchase our raw materials from environmentally friendly sources. The wind power initiative takes our current environmental strategy to an exciting new level. Our customers really appreciate our efforts to preserve the environment."

With over 45 years in the furniture industry, Classic Comfort is one of New Mexico's largest furniture manufacturers, with their products sold through a world-wide network of distributors and retailers. These distribution and retail partners have also embraced the Green House program, by following Classic Comfort's lead and adopting similar wind power and environmentally friendly initiatives across their businesses.

"Classic Comfort provided us with a series of webinars that showed us how we could optimize our green efforts within our retail stores," explains Roy Carter, owner of a 5-location furniture chain in Ohio. "Our customers now have the ability to purchase environmentally friendly furnishings that also look beautiful in their homes. They love the fact that their kitchen table was produced with wind power. It's good for the environment and it's good for business."

For more information about Classic Comfort Furnishings and their wind power program, please contact Mark Simmons at Classic Comfort; (555) 987-1234.

#

The sample press release about Classic Comfort has been provided for your review. While the content is fictitious, it includes the standard format rules of a press release. Consider copying this format as you write your own press release.

After the initial paragraph, which covers the Who, What, Where, Why, When and How, subsequent paragraphs should contain extra pertinent facts, or quotes that serve to advance the story. Finally, in the last paragraph, you can add some fluff about your company, like the number of years you have been in business, a brief overview of your products and services, and your phone number or web address for additional information about the story or your company. The writers and editors will cut your story from the bottom up, so the core of your story must be covered within the first one or two paragraphs.

The newspapers, magazines, and Internet news services are looking to fill spaces within their publications. They may have small spaces that are available, or large holes that need to be filled. Depending on the space they need to fill, they may elect to add a simple excerpt from your press release or include the entire story word-for-word. As you write your press release, make sure it can stand as a one-paragraph blurb, or a full article. If the publication likes your story, your press release could become a feature article. This is equivalent to hitting a home run in the public relations world. In this case, the editor or writer will most likely contact you to set up an interview to gather more story details. They may also send a photographer over to your office to take some pictures to use in the article.

This is another opportunity to make the editor's job easy. Always include a selection of clear, simple, relevant, high-resolution, professional-quality photographs for their use with the press release. Once again, you are making their job easier and helping them to fill holes and gaps within their publication. The publications will often run your photograph, with a few simple lines below, rather than using the text provided within your press release. Celebrate if they elect to do this, as a picture is worth a thousand words, to both your business and the publication.

Press Kits: Press kits are designed to make the writer or editor's job as easy as possible. They can contain the lead press release, additional facts, and a thorough history of your company, with profiles of key executives. The press kit will also include digital files of all of the text elements, with a collection of professional, high-quality photographs to choose from. This makes it very easy for the publication to run with your story. Often the press kit will include more details about the story, other examples of the company's community involvement, and past articles that have covered the company or similar stories. The editor may not wish to run your lead press release, but he could find an interesting angle that will appeal to their specific readership within your press kit.

Press kits come in all shapes and sizes. Some press kits are glossy and glamorous, with cutting-edge graphics and audio / visual effects. Other press kits are very simple, with a corporate pocket folder containing the press release, the company contact information, a brief company history, and a disc containing the photographs and text files. I have seen elaborate kits, including bottles of wine with specially printed labels, gift baskets filled with food, tickets to sports and special events, and presents of all types. Clearly it is to your benefit to find favor in the eyes of your local press contacts, but these tactics can be viewed as inappropriate or over-the-top. Any special gifts should be provided to advance the story, not to buy coverage – once again, they will direct you to the advertising sales department if they believe you are over-promoting your company. Mix your generosity with a heavy dose of practical wisdom, and be sure that your swag has a purpose that helps advance the story, catches the editor's attention, or brings some humor and personality to your press kit.

For example, if you own the local minor league hockey team and you just signed an exciting new player, including a pair of tickets for the writer to visit the ice and watch the talents of your new addition is absolutely appropriate. The publication will appreciate access to the venue and will be in a better position to cover the story.

I handled the marketing for a national retail company that specialized in packaging and shipping parcels for consumers and businesses. As you can imagine, we did a great deal of packaging and shipping during the weeks leading up to Christmas. We sent our press kits out in our professionally packaged shipping boxes. The boxes would arrive and the reporters would always open them, believing them to be a holiday gift from a friend or family member.

When they opened our kits, they would find a cleverly packaged lead press release, usually focused on our holiday charity program. We also included a collection of photos, important packaging tips for the holidays, critical shipping deadlines, and interesting facts about shipping volumes, best-price carrier options, and ideas for hot, inexpensive gifts. For a few years, we packaged fragile ornaments within the press kits and explained within our cover letter how we packaged the ornaments to arrive safely, allowing the writer to convey the same tips to their readers. Our press kits were always a big hit and they often found their way into articles and news stories.

Press Contacts: It is very important to send your press kits and press releases to the correct person within the publication. The business editor is a good place to start, but your particular article may be better received by a local columnist or feature writer that covers articles similar to your topic.

It is important to introduce yourself to the editors, writers, and columnists at local, trade, and national publications. If they know you and are familiar with your company, they will trust the press releases that you send to them and will often print them. I have built networks of reporters and editors who would almost always print my press releases. However, I had to do my homework, meet them in person, follow up on the phone, and always write press releases that contained meaningful, interesting stories, and were not straight commercials about my company.

Public Relations Companies: Public relations firms specialize in press contacts. In fact, when you engage a public relations firm, you are essentially buying their press contacts, as well as their expertise. They are adept at building press kits, writing press releases, introducing the winning angles, and managing their important contacts across the country. Over the years, I have hired, and fired, many public relations firms. I have also brought PR in-house and managed it internally, without the support of a PR firm. Both approaches can work well.

At times, I have worked with extremely gifted and creative PR experts. They are worth their weight in gold. However, public relations firms often receive a bad reputation for taking high retainer fees and not producing consistent results. Before you hire a PR firm, it is important to recognize that PR is not an exact science. Public Relations firms can do a terrific job, but they cannot guarantee that a publication will run your story. It takes patience, persistence, timing, and a little bit of luck. However, I have found that there are ways to keep your public relations firms on a performance schedule that ensures that they are providing good value for your investment. Here are a few ideas:

- **PR Calendar:** Work with your public relations firm to develop a public relations calendar that spells out all of their activities for the year, or the term of your agreement. The calendar should include a schedule of press releases, articles, features, and events that work together to accomplish your objects, just like your marketing calendar. Discuss the PR Calendar weekly with your agency contacts and be sure to keep them on track.

- **Clear Objectives:** Be sure to state your objectives clearly and in writing with your public relations firm. Discuss these objectives at every meeting and get updates on how the progress is coming along. If your goal is to be on the front page of the Wall Street Journal, then be sure to make this clear to your PR firm. They may believe that they are doing a terrific job in just getting frequent mentions in your local papers.

- **Weekly Meetings:** Set a weekly meeting or conference call with your public relations company. These meetings do not have to be very long, but they will serve to hold everyone accountable, keep the calendar on track, and ensure that everyone is working toward the same objectives.

- **Press Clippings or Summaries:** Your public relations firm should be building a file of the press you are receiving. Maintain a file of all of the articles and develop a tracking chart to count the number of lines of press your company is receiving each week. These figures can be added to your PR metrics and the articles can be linked to your website press room.

- **Additional Metrics:** In addition to counting the lines of press you receive each week, you will want to develop additional metrics for attributing leads and sales to your public relations activities. There are easy ways to do this – I will cover just three here, and I am sure that you can come up with additional ways to establish PR metrics within your company.

Dedicated Landing Pages: Develop a series of unique landing pages that correspond only to your PR activities. Do not promote these landing pages and URLs in any other place or marketing vehicle, but mention them only in your press releases and list them only in your press materials. Additionally, do not provide any other web addresses or URLs that are not among the dedicated list you have developed for PR purposes. For example, do not list your main web address within any of your press materials. This will allow you to attribute all of the hits that you receive on these PR dedicated landing pages to your public relations activities. I acknowledge that this is not a perfect system. Members of the press will still visit your main web page via search engines and other methods, and non-press related leads will find your landing pages the same way. However, the majority of hits to these landing pages can be credited to your PR activities and, over time, you will have meaningful metrics with which to assess the results of your investment in this marketing tactic.

Exclusive E-Mail Addresses: Just as you can develop unique landing pages for your public relations activities, you can list e-mail addresses that are exclusive to you public relations materials. In-bound inquiries to these e-mail addresses can be counted and assessed, just as you count hits to your unique landing pages.

Unique Call Tracking Numbers: We reviewed call tracking in an earlier chapter. Just as call tracking systems can be used to evaluate each of your marketing tactics, or discern what advertisements in which publications are working best, call tracking numbers can be provided within all of your press materials. By using these dedicated, unique numbers within your press materials, you can attribute any lead or sale that results from calls to your PR numbers to your PR activities. It is important to only use these numbers within your PR materials, while not allowing your standard phone numbers to appear in any press release, press kit, or landing page that is dedicated to PR activities.

At first, these tracking mechanisms will not yield great results but, over time, you will be able to develop metrics that directly track the results of your public relations activities and give your PR firm, or in-house efforts, the credit that they deserve.

- **Be Flexible:** Public relations firms are famous for their crazy ideas. They are gifted at thinking outside the box and playing with different story angles. You may not like or support some of their ideas, but you need to be flexible and willing to give their creative ideas a try. You are paying these individuals for their creative energies, so don't hold them to a set of conventions that could limit their success. Just be sure that their proposals are inline with your corporate brand and image.

- **Be Accessible:** It is also important to be accessible to your public relations firm. Be available to talk directly to the press, ready to appear in broadcast interviews, and willing to participate in photo shoots. Don't put these people off with your busy schedule. If necessary, give them access to you on a few weekends, so they can quickly assemble the materials they need for a professional press kit.

Notify your public relations team of your travel plans. They can often take advantage of your travel schedule to arrange interviews with local and regional publications. They can schedule photos of your meetings, store tours, and trade show events. Many of these activities offer compelling story angles that will appeal to the destination press, as well as the publications back home.

Share important corporate accomplishments with your PR people. Let them know about new customers, projects, contracts, and hires. Many of these events will translate into good material for stories and articles.

Standing For Something: It is important that your company stands for something beyond simply making money. Giving back to the community is an important role for every company. Select one or two charities or community causes and align your company with them. Donate proceeds, host events, sponsor activities, and volunteer your staff to support your charity partners. Whether you are dedicated to a sustainable environment, focused on finding a cure for cancer, eager to support the troops, or passionate about literacy, your company needs to stand for something that is larger than itself.

I suggest that you select one or two causes to embrace consistently and thoroughly, rather than supporting a wide variety of organizations. This will allow you to focus your staff's energies on the charity's event calendar and find ways to work with them to help them accomplish their goals. You will see more results and will be more closely aligned with a cause if you are consistent and focused.

Relationships: Just as your PR firm maintains important contacts within the press, it is important for you to build and maintain key relationships within your industry, the community, and the press. These people are the movers and shakers, the commercial influencers, and linked to the well-connected within your industry. Invite them to tour your facilities, include them in your events, get to know them over lunch, and keep them posted on your accomplishments.

With tools like LinkedIn, Facebook, and Twitter, it is easier than ever to maintain these relationships with your key contacts.

Establish an Industry Expert: Industries need people to step forward and be the expert spokesperson for the community of companies that comprise the industry. The press wants to make a few, quick phone calls to key players to get reactions on new legislation and events. The tradeshow companies want a high-profile testimonial for the success of the latest show. Local universities and the community are looking for speakers that can inform students and the public on important industry trends. The industry trade publications want to quote and follow key players that have the pulse of the market within their grasp and current statistics at their fingertips.

Identify someone within your organization to be your key spokesperson for the industry. He can come from engineering, accounting, marketing, customer service or business development. Ask him to attend the key industry happenings, make special appearances at public events, host informative seminars, write a series of articles, and be quoted regularly in your press releases. Introduce your industry expert to all of the trade publication editors and writers and clearly convey where their expertise lies. Ask him to track trends within the industry, contact their counterparts at other companies within the industry - including your competitors - and know what is going on with the changing needs of key industry customers.

It does not take long to establish a company representative. He will become a lighting rod for your organization and, if he remains active within the industry, he will soon become a key industry spokesperson. As a result, your company will become the default expert, or the gold standard, for your industry and you will garner the lion's share of the press attention.

Key Tactics for Public Relations: There are many terrific tactics that can be used within your public relations plans. All of these should be included within your marketing plan, added to your calendar, and receive allocations from your budget. I have touched on many of these proven tactics within this chapter, but I want to be sure that they are not missed within the context of another topic. While the following list is not complete, it will provide you with a good start as you develop your public relations plan:

PR Tactics:

- Consistently Send Press Releases to Key Publications
- Send Press Releases to your Customers
- Write Articles for Local and Industry Publications based on your Area of Interest or Expertise
- Develop Key Press Contacts with Local and Industry Publications
- Develop a Press Kit

- Sponsor Industry Events
- Build a Network of Key Community and Industry Relationships
- Support and Become Active with a Charity or Cause
- Host Seminars, Workshops and Classes
- Host a Grand Opening or Open House
- Create Annual or Quarterly Promotional Events
- Identify An Industry Expert within your Organization
- Form and Promote Strategic Partnerships
- Develop Seasonal Promotions
- Create a Scholarship Program for Local Schools / Universities
- Hold Press Events and Announcements
- Host or Enter Industry Competitions
- Develop a Series of YouTube Videos
- Donate Your Staff's Time to Support a Local Event or Charity

As you can see, public relations do not need to be complicated or intimidating. Rather, PR tactics should be deployed consistently within the context of your marketing plan. Most public relations activities are inexpensive and extremely cost-effective. When you add a good dose of public relations to your marketing matrix, you will stretch your marketing dollars dramatically to help you accomplish your goals. With some dedicated brainstorming, a focus on interesting story angles, cultivation of your key contacts, and consistent application of your public relations calendar, you will develop a winning public relations formula that will enhance your corporate image, establish your role within the industry, and attract new customers and business opportunities.

CHAPTER 14:
CUSTOMER RETENTION PROGRAMS

Customers.

There is no asset more valuable. No endeavor more critical. No business investment more worthwhile.

Customers are the lifeblood of your company. We discussed this thoroughly in *Chapter 4: Defining Your Customer*. However, the focus of that earlier chapter was understanding who your customers are. The focus of this chapter is how to keep the customers you have.

It is important to know the value of your customers. In previous chapters, we had an example in which we calculated the actual dollar value of a customer. We will revise the concept with a new example.

If your company has annual sales of $3,500,000 and you have 850 active customers in your database, then each customer is worth an average of $4,117 per year to your business ($3,500,000 / 850 = $4,117). This is a significant sum. Each customer has tremendous value to your business.

Speaking of your business, let's figure out what your actual value per customer is for your business now.

Calculate this figure for your business:

Total Annual Sales / Number of Customers = Value per Customer

Your Total Annual Sales: $

÷

Your Number of Customers:

=

Your Value per Customer: $

What did you come up with? Is it a significant sum? Is it worth keeping each customer happy? Are you interested in retaining every customer, based on their incremental value to your business? The answer to these questions is likely a resounding "Yes"!

Going back to our example, if last year's marketing budget was $85,000, and you generated 235 new customers, your average cost per new customer is $361.

In this example, you are investing $361 dollars to generate a single new customer, and that customer has an average value of $4,117. This is a terrific value proposition for your business - one that is certainly worth repeating.

Now let's calculate your actual cost per new customer, based on last year's budget and sales performance. For a more precise figure, you can use the average of your figures for the last several years, if these numbers are available to you.

Calculate this figure for your business:

Annual Marketing Budget / Number of New Customers = Cost Per New Customer

Annual Marketing Budget: $

÷

Number of New Customers:

=

Cost per New Customer: $

How much higher is your value per customer, when compared to your cost per new customer? If there is not a significant difference, then you have a marketing challenge. However, this challenge can be overcome by implementing the fundamentals of Formula Marketing.

If your value per customer is significantly higher than your cost per new customer, then you have a terrific value proposition that should encourage you to accelerate the growth of your marketing budget. Either way, I believe you will agree that it is extremely important to retain your existing customers.

Now let's consider how much it will cost to retain, or keep, each of these valuable customers. We will find that it will cost a great deal more money to find new customers than to keep your current customers. Your cost per new customer can form your budget limit for your customer retention strategy, meaning that you should not spend much more to retain an existing customer than you would spend to attract a new customer. In this example, if your cost to retain a new customer exceeds $361, you could be better off focusing your energies on bringing in new customers. However, the high cost of retaining an existing customer is more likely a reflection of a misallocation of your marketing funds. It should not be expensive to retain each existing customer. In fact, you will find that an investment of $10, $25, or $40 per customer should be more than enough to keep your customers happy and coming back.

It is important to add customer retention to your marketing strategies and to develop a series of proven tactics that carry out those strategies. Additionally, you will want to develop core customer retention objectives and the metrics needed to assess the effectiveness of your tactics. A customer retention program should be a key component to your marketing plan and a fixture within your marketing matrix. In short, keeping your customers happy should be an important part of your marketing formula.

That will be the focus of this chapter.

Customer Service Programs: Given the value of each customer, it is imperative to have a customer service program in place for your business. Each employee should have a clear understanding of the value of a customer and the efforts they are allowed to make in order to keep each customer happy.

Rather than develop a customer service manual that few will ever read, have a series of meetings with your staff to discuss the value of the customer. During these meetings, brainstorm for ideas to keep each customer happy. Your staff will create some terrific ideas. They will also learn what they can and cannot do to keep a customer happy. As they help you develop strategies and tactics to retain your current customers, they will begin to appreciate the value of each customer and the remedies available to them for supporting the needs of each customer.

As part of these meetings, consider including a few of these topics:

Returns: What do you say when a customer wants to return the item that they purchased? How do you handle the situation now? Do you provide a full refund, a partial refund, provide them with a new item of equal value, or do you ask the customer to tell you what they would like you to do to resolve the situation? Discuss these situations openly with your staff, so they know exactly what to do. Customers generally want their issues resolved immediately, so empower your employees to handle these issues directly with your customers and to their 100% satisfaction.

Complaints: How do you currently handle customer complaints? Do you keep records on the number and nature of complaints that you have? Do you have policies in place to resolve complaints, or handle them on a case-by-case basis? Do additional people get involved if there are customer complaints? How do you handle a really angry customer? At what point do you suggest the customer take their business somewhere else? It is very helpful to your staff to discuss the parameters available to them to handle customer complaints.

Special Requests: Every business has systems in place and they are important to follow. Without systems, your business will be less efficient, waste a great deal of money, and will not be able to process a large volume of transactions. Customers will occasionally make requests that cause you to alter or abandon your systems. How will you accommodate these requests? Will you allow a staff member to change the system in order to support a special customer request? Are there dollar limits for breaking the system? Is there an approval process in place that allows for these events? Special requests are inevitable. So it is a good idea to train your employees and key team members how to handle them to the customer's satisfaction, without diminishing the systems or the efficiency of your company.

Follow Up: How do you follow up with a customer? Do you send them a thank-you note when they make a substantial purchase? Do you follow up with an angry customer and confirm that they are 100% satisfied with their purchase and experience? If an item is returned, what do you do to understand the reason for the return? Do you follow-up on the quality of the item, the process used to create it, or try to discover a pattern in the return of the item or service?

Referrals: Do you have a formal program in place for handling customer referrals? Do you ask your customers for referrals? Do you thank them when they refer someone to your business? For example, our family dentist always sends us tickets to the movies to thank us when we refer a friend to their practice. Do you track the number of referrals you receive to your business? Referrals are the easiest and most powerful way to build your business. It is very important to have a customer referral program as part of your marketing plan.

These are just a few things to consider as you begin to develop your customer retention programs. Be sure to get everyone involved in developing the program. If your whole company is involved in the development of your customer retention program, you will have a much easier time implementing and maintaining the program successfully.

Customer Database: Your marketing formula should always begin with tactics focused around your existing customers. Your best dollars are invested with the people who have already done business with you. They have demonstrated that they need your products and services, understand your value proposition, know where you are located, and are comfortable with your staff and processes.

One of the best ways to stay in touch with your customers on a regular basis is with a customer database. The database does not need to be complicated. It can simply contain each customer's name, e-mail address, physical address, phone number, and a few notes; like what they have purchased, their birthdays, and what they spend with you each year. There are many terrific database programs available, like ACT!, Pipeline Deals, SalesForce.com, and Goldmine. The feature you need most is the ability to export your customer database as a csv or excel file.

This will allow you to easily customize and address your direct mail pieces, e-blasts, holiday cards, birthday cards, cross-selling pieces, and service reminders.

I am always surprised when a client does not have an updated or well-maintained customer database. This is the most important tangible asset of your business, as it is your only lasting link to your customers, which are the source of your revenue and future growth. However, I have found that most businesses do not do a good job of maintaining their customer database. During any meeting that I have with a client, the conversation will always cover the status of their customer database because, as I have said, that is where I believe you need to start your marketing planning.

When I ask about their customer database, my clients generally squirm in their chairs, offer quick excuses, or avoid eye contact. Some brave clients will boldly state that they do a great job in maintaining their customer database. However, when I need to use it to execute a campaign, or begin to dig beneath the surface, we quickly find that the database is obsolete, out-of-date, inaccurate, or in a format that cannot be used.

The Power of a Customer Database: Customer databases, when maintained, are a powerful tool within your marketing plan. They give you the ability to send out monthly newsletters, regular e-blasts, news articles about your business or industry, new product and service releases, and allow you to make good, old-fashioned sales calls, whether in person or over the phone. A good customer database will help you remember your customers on their birthdays, important anniversaries, and during special holidays. You can remind your customers of special sales events and new product launches, and provide them with incentives to return to your business throughout the year. You can thank your customers for their business each year with a coupon book, a special offer, or honor them for their patronage. You can also provide them with small gifts, promotional items, and seasonal gifts throughout the year.

All of these touches and follow-ups will result in customers who feel appreciated, are well-informed of your product line, familiar with your business, and empowered to visit often and tell their friends and neighbors. These actions, when applied consistently and professionally within the parameters of your company brand and image, will yield incredible results. You will set yourself apart from the competition, increase your number of transactions, boost your average ticket per customer, generate more referrals, increase your margins, and drive more revenue.

The best thing about customer retention programs is that they are relatively inexpensive to maintain. A simple thank-you letter, postcard, or small gift does not have to cost a lot of money. Additionally, your response rates when mailing special offers to your customer database are significantly higher than when you mail to a purchased list, or a list of prospective customers who have not done business with you. The statistics are clear:

7% Response Rate when mailing to Current Customer Database

0.25% Response Rate when mailing to Purchased Mailing List

A difference of 6.75% in rate of return is a big difference in the marketing world! These statistics from the Direct Marketing Association suggest that the average response rate when mailing to your customer database are a full 7%, while response rates for mailing to new prospects who are unfamiliar with your business are approximately a quarter of 1%. These results will vary, based on the offers that you use within your campaigns. However, suffice it to say that you will receive significantly higher returns on your investment when you mail to a database of current customers than to a group of strangers.

Knowing that an average response rate of 7% is possible, when you mail to your current customer database, shows that there is real gold in those hills. Meaning that you can develop a series of programs, campaigns, and customer retention strategies that are designed to drive high margin revenue on a regular basis. Here is an example:

Example: Sunshine Garden Center – Potting Soil Campaign

Step 1: Dirt Bags, Inc. is a key supplier to Sunshine Garden Center. Dirt Bags offers discounted bags of potting soil to Sunshine Garden Center. Cost: $5.00 per bag.

Step 2: Sunshine Garden Center contacts Dirt Bags, Inc. and requests co-op dollars to promote the discounted potting soil to their VIP customers. Dirt Bags agrees to provide $500 toward the effort, if Sunshine will purchase a minimum of 350 bags of potting soil. Sunshine Garden Center agrees.

Step 3: Sunshine Garden Center designs a campaign to their customer database of 2,500 people, offering discounted bags of potting soil for $7.00 to All VIP customers, limit four per customer. The direct mail piece is a glossy postcard, printed 8.5" X 11" and folded to 8.5" X 5.5", with a creative design that will appeal to the VIP customers and is consistent with Sunshine's corporate branding. The piece explains that the regular price for the potting soil is $15.00 and the coupon must be brought in to realize the amazing deal, while supplies last.

The cost of the campaign follows:

Graphic Design:	$ 400
Printing:	$1,100
Postage:	$ 650
Sub Total:	$2,150

Co-Op Dollars Applied: <u><$ 500></u>
Total Cost: **$1,650**

Postage Note: Cost based on Pre-Sort Standard Class; 2,500 pieces @ $0.26 each

Step 4: The campaign is mailed out strategically to arrive on Thursday, just prior to the weekend, so Sunshine VIP customers will be more likely to use the coupon. It is a limited time offer and, within two weeks, 7% of the 2,500 VIP customers, or 175 people, arrive to redeem the coupons and purchase the potting soil.

Step 5: Resulting Metrics: Of course, the VIP customers are ready to get to work in their gardens. They need more supplies than just the potting soil. They buy other items, as well. The results follow in the example below:

Potting Soil Campaign Results:
(1) Number of Coupon Redeemed: 175
(2) Average # of Bags of Potting Soil Purchased By Customer: 2
(3) Total Bags Purchased: 350
(4) Total Gross Profit: $700
(5) Total "Other" Sales Resulting Directly from Campaign: $5,075
(6) Gross Profit on "Other Sales" After COGS: $3,045
(7) Total Gross Profit After COGS (4 + 6): $3,745
(8) Cost of Campaign: $1,650

Total Gross Profit from Campaign (7 – 8): $2,905

This was a successful campaign. If Sunshine Garden Center ran a similar campaign every month, they would generate a great deal more business, drive greater profits and turn their customer database into a powerful profit center. The key to successful campaigns like this one is maintaining your customer database so you can leverage its power.

Disciplined Systems: When it comes to selling your business or handing over the reins to your replacement, the customer database is germane to the value of your business and to your role within the company. This is not a revolutionary concept. Most business people understand the value of a customer database. What is so surprising is how few people actually do a good job of maintaining their databases in a usable format. Never before have there been so many tools to build, maintain and leverage your client database. So why is it an area of regret and embarrassment for so many companies?

I think the core of the issue revolves around discipline and systems. It takes time and energy to maintain a customer database. You need to enter the data before forgetting to do so. You always believe that you will have an opportunity to enter the data later. However, we are always busy with the next deal, the next transaction, or the next customer. The key is developing a system that enforces a disciplined approach to maintaining your customer database. Whether you develop a technology-based system that captures names and addresses through a point of purchase register, enter every business card you receive into a CRM before you begin your work day, or ask your customers to fill out a simple form, you need to develop a fixed system that will facilitate the building of your database.

There are many fun ways to develop your customer database. You can have a contest and give away some of your products and services. Each customer can fill out a simple form, or drop their business card into a drawing box.

When I interviewed the Surf Brothers for the earlier chapter on differentiation, they were in the process of building their customer database by offering a drawing for a big screen TV. They wanted to be able to e-mail special offers to their customers on a regular basis, and cross-promote their catering services during different times of the year. So they developed a promotion to trade the chance to win a big screen TV for their customer's e-mail addresses. Many of their customers accepted their proposal and The Surf Brothers developed a comprehensive e-mail list.

Hosting a survey is also a great way to learn about your customers, your service level, and your product mix. You can also learn your customer's contact information and add them easily to your database. This can be done on your website, in person, or within your retail locations.

If customers pay you by check, make copies of each check and enter their name and address into your database. Some point of sale systems allow you to gain this information through receiving the credit card data, as well. The point is, there are many ways to retain a customer's contact information. The key is adding it to your customer database and then leveraging the power of that database.

Develop a VIP Club or Loyalty Program: Many of my restaurant clients have a VIP or customer loyalty program in place. These programs can be applied to many different kinds of businesses. The concept is simple. In exchange for their name and address, the customer receives VIP or club membership with special offers, special access to exclusive products and services, interesting insider information, and special pricing. Generally, the customer will save money over the course of the year by joining a loyalty program.

These customers can become incredibly loyal, a terrific source of referrals, and the core of your recurring revenue. You can tap their spending power at any time and bring them into your business during quiet seasons, slow days or less productive times. These customers are also where you begin when you launch a new product or service. They are your early adopters, your focus group, or your initial sales force. You can empower your VIP Club members with personalized flyers, coupon books, or special offer cards. Give them a mission to tell the world about your company, and every coupon or offer that returns with their personal code gives them a discount, commission, or merchandise for their efforts. Some loyalty programs are highly sophisticated and can provide thousands of dollars in savings for the customers that join them.

Can you design a loyalty program for your business? Are their ways that you can empower your best customers to generate more referrals for your business? Can you develop a program that directly benefits your best customers and keeps them coming back for many years?

Get the staff together and discuss the best ways to build your customer database and how to use it once it is built. Discuss creating a VIP Club or loyalty program. How would it work? Who would it benefit? How would you promote it? You may come to find that a customer loyalty program is the best element within your marketing matrix.

Learn Your Customers Names: People love to hear their own names. This is one of the foundational concepts introduced in Dale Carnegie's *How to Win Friends and Influence People* (which is a must-read for any marketing professional or business owner). You will gain loyal, regular customers by greeting them warmly each time you see them, using their first name. They will be less likely to go to your competition. They will view you as a friend, a trusted ally, a critical resource. It is difficult to remember hundreds of names, but consider the value of each customer. If each customer is worth several hundred or several thousand dollars a year to your business, then remembering their names is a worthwhile endeavor.

You may have hundreds of staff members and thousands of customers, so the prospect of learning everyone's name may seem daunting. However, there are ways to develop systems to do this. Your staff will have ideas, devices, and systems that they use currently. Tap these valuable people to assist in the development of a name campaign. The results will astound you.

Learn Your Customers Interests: In addition to learning your customer's name, take it a step further and make the effort to learn their interests. This is Sales 101. Get your customers talking about themselves and they will believe that you are a fascinating conversationalist! Often remembering a few key factoids about a person will assist you in remembering their names. An easy way to do this is to ask them what they did last weekend, or what their plans are for the upcoming weekend. You will learn a great deal about your customers by asking these simple questions. Are they into sports, family, theatre, camping, or cars? Soon you will develop a series of topics to converse about, articles to share, and common interests that will draw you closer together.

Why are these customer relationships so important? Because your products and services are available at lower prices, closer locations, better terms and, possibly, with better service at your competitors or on the Internet. Your relationship with your customers is the real reason they continue to do business with you. For this reason, you need to excel at your customer relationships. Turn them into close friends and they will rarely leave your business for a lower price.

Customer Retention Program: Example

In concluding this chapter, we will review an example of a customer retention program.

Play Time Toys is located within a grocery-anchored shopping center in an upscale community. They have a large location with a good selection of high-quality toys and books for children. Their prices are higher than the local big box retailers, but they cater to a clientele that places a premium on their time and the experience of buying toys for their children and grandchildren.

When Play Time opened this new location, they knew building their customer retention program would be critical to their long-term success. This is how they did it.

Beginning at their grand opening, Play Time offered a contest drawing for three $100 gift certificates to anyone who visited their store. Customers filled out a simple form for a chance to win the prize. The form asked for their name, address, e-mail, and phone number so they could notify the winners. During the grand opening, 250 people entered the drawing to win the gift certificates. The Play Time Toys customer retention strategy was in business.

Play Time Toys then developed a monthly newsletter. The newsletter featured hot new toys that would appeal to both boys and girls, as well as educational toys that would appeal to their parents and grandparents. The newsletters were printed and mailed to the 250 contacts on the contest list, and an html version was e-mailed to the same list, with links to special landing pages that allowed Play Time Toys to track click-thrus to their website. Extra newsletters were printed as part of the print run and distributed at the counter of the store, and from a newsstand directly in front of the grocery store. The newsletter featured coupons focused on bringing their new and prospective customers back to the store, which Play Time used to track response.

Additionally, Playtime acquired a 2,500 name direct mail list of all of the homes within a 3-mile radius showing the presence of children, and high net-worth homeowners over the age of 55 years of age (grandparents). A map was inserted within the newsletters, along with a few additional deeper discount coupons and an announcement of their recent opening. When each of the coupons was redeemed, Play Time stapled a second copy of the receipt to each redeemed coupon and then began to track their metrics for the success of each offer, and the total sales resulting from each coupon. The address of the recipient appeared on the back of each coupon, so the identity of each customer was linked to their purchase.

When a customer visited the store, Play Time Toys staff members were trained to invite the children to join the Play Time Birthday Club, where kids would receive a small catalog with special offers three weeks prior to their birthday. One week prior to their birthday, the children also received a digitally printed greeting card, customized with their name inside, with an invitation to visit Play Time Toys to receive a free birthday gift. Inserted within the birthday card was a special gift card for the parents, with a 20% discount coupon for any purchase within the store. The redeemed birthday gifts and discount cards were also carefully tracked by Play Time staff members.

Additionally, Play Time Toys offered a sweepstakes for $25, $50, and $100 gift certificates to every customer that visited the store. The ongoing contest offered prize drawings every month, and an average of 300 new customers entered the drawing with their name, address, e-mail, and phone number.

Within three months, the Play Time Toys customer list grew to 1,200 people, while they continued to use the acquired prospective customer list of 2,500 people for the surrounding community. However, they were careful to ensure that any duplicate names between the two lists were deleted from the prospective customer list.

Play Time Toys continued to mail and e-mail the monthly newsletter. However, the 1,200 proven customers were given an opportunity to join the Play Time Parents Club, to receive on-going discounts of 10% on any purchase and advance notice of the release and availability of new toys. Meanwhile, the children were encouraged to join the Birthday Club, as well as the new Saturday Afternoon Playtime Club, where club members were invited to the store to demo new toys, attend Lego workshops and tea parties, read stories, learn more about the dolls and stuffed animals in the store and, of course, play.

The members of the Parents Club, Birthday Club, Saturday Club, and anyone else on the customer list were also sent a special red envelop with their name and a code printed on it. The red envelopes were also printed with "Prize Inside, Open Only at Play Time Toys". A personalized letter requested that the recipient give the red envelope to a neighbor, classmate, or friend who had never been to Play Time Toys before, with special instructions not to open the letter until they were at the store. The customers of Play Time Toys would be entered into a special contest for a free $100 gift certificate if the red envelope they gave to their friend was returned to the store and the code number was entered into the contest drawing. Meanwhile, the person receiving the red envelope would receive one of 5 prizes, some very small and inexpensive, and a few larger, more expensive prizes. Once inside the store, the new customers were invited to enter the monthly gift certificate drawing, the Birthday Club, the Parents Club, and the Saturday Club.

Within six months, Play Time Toys grew their customer list to over 2,500 names. Using this list, and the acquired mailing list (with duplicates to the customer list removed), Play Time Toys mailed out their Holiday Catalog in the second week of September, just after school started, with special back-to-school offers and coupons. A second Holiday Catalog was mailed just before Halloween, with special spooky Halloween offers. Finally, a third Holiday Catalog was mailed just after Thanksgiving, with special Holiday offers and coupons.

All of the coupons were unique and contained tracking codes that could be easily added to the metrics chart so the number of coupons redeemed and the total sales generated could be tracked.

By the end of the year, the Play Time Toys customer list grew to 4,000 names. Using the saved sales receipts for each customer (remember that each coupon has the customer's name and address printed on the back, so their purchase is linked to their name, the Play Time Toys staff now knew what toys each of the kids and parents on the list were buying. They were now able to notify the parents and kids when a new toy within that line was available and they were able to cross-promote similar toys and books that would appeal to those kids. Using this data, Play Time Toys continued to promote, cross-sell, and encourage their customers to return again and again.

Play Time Toys then launched an interactive website geared for children and parents. The website contained PDF versions of past newsletters, toy catalogs, and special offers. The website also acted as a play portal, with links to the toy manufacturer websites, product reviews, and news about toys. Play Time Toys also added special web pages with information and photos of the Birthday Club, the Parent's Club, and the Saturday Club. Within these pages were forms that could be filled out to join each club, with special offers and contests for new members.

Within their first year of business, Play Time Toys built a large customer database, gathered metrics on every offer, developed several special clubs, and created an effective customer retention strategy. Going forward, if sales ever begin to decline, the shopping center decides to embark on a messy remodel, or a competitor opens nearby, Play Time Toys is in a strong strategic position, with the ability to leverage its proven customer database in times of need.

This is just one example. You can build a similar retention program for your customers. Get together with your staff and discuss how you can build your customer list, encourage your customers to spend with you more often, cross-promote different products and services, and provide incentives to refer you to their friends and contacts. The key to a successful customer retention program is developing a disciplined, formulaic approach, with mechanisms to gain addresses, track results, and build your database. Over time, you can develop a powerful customer retention program that is designed to maintain your sales levels, while reaching new potential customers.

CHAPTER 15:
CORPORATE SALES DEPARTMENTS

Sales is a part of marketing. It falls under the marketing umbrella of strategies and tactics. If you have a sales department for your business, it must be viewed as one of your core marketing tactics. It may be the most productive tactic within your marketing matrix, as it is for many companies.

This is not to say that the director of marketing should run the sales department. Most marketing people are not gifted sales people and lack the skill set to run a sales department. However, marketing must interface closely with sales and have oversight on several critical areas. A summary follows:

Sales Processes: The marketing department should work with the sales department to design the sales processes. The CMO must decide how sales leads will be generated, whether through direct sales, advertising, marketing, public relations, or all of these methods. The sales process must be understood by the marketing team so they can develop the steps for (1) when a lead is generated, (2) the language and methods used in the selling process (3) the process by which the prospect gathers key information to make an informed decision, (4) the client purchase process, (5) how the client is supported after the purchase, (6) how the client is cross-sold additional products and services and, finally, (7) how the client is involved in the referral program. There are important corporate materials and branding opportunities within each step of the sales process, and marketing must be active with every step.

Generating Sales Leads: The marketing department should be charged with the responsibility for generating sales leads. They must select the strategies and tactics that will generate the highest quality leads at the lowest possible cost per lead. Sales should have an active voice in all of these decisions and should communicate often with marketing regarding the quality of leads, quantity of leads, source of leads, and the methods used to advance each lead to a sale.

Sales Metrics: Metrics must be developed by marketing to track lead generation across all tactics. Marketing should also track close ratios for each lead source, so they understand which lead sources close most often and which leads make the best clients. Marketing should also have a thorough understanding of the close ratio of each sales person and the methods used for best success. Best practices need to be communicated to the entire sales team often and thoroughly so the lowest performing sales people emulate their more productive peers, and the best sales people learn more effective techniques to continue their success. Marketing should track and maintain all of the sales metrics and provide them often (daily, weekly, monthly, quarterly, annually) to the sales manager and, if appropriate, the each member of the sales team.

Sales Collateral: The marketing department should be responsible for the development of the sales tool kit. All of the advertisements, press releases, direct mail pieces, sales collateral (like brochures, sales sheets, presentation folders), client materials, forms, e-mail signatures, sales aids, landing pages, the website, and the product packaging should fall within the roles and responsibilities of the marketing department. Marketing must understand the needs of the sales department and communicate with them daily to understand what materials are needed, how they are used, and what is most effective.

Sales Presentations: Marketing should develop all of the sales presentation materials to support the sales function. Marketing needs to design the branding and images used in the PowerPoint presentations, online demonstrations, webinars, seminars, meetings, product demonstrations and open houses. Marketing should help craft the language, the steps of the presentation, the scripting, and the steps within the agenda. Marketing should also work with sales to establish the responsibilities of Sales for lead generation, follow-up, data collection for each prospect, and the next steps of the sales process.

Sales Materials for Trade Shows: While sales people generally run the booth during the trade shows, the marketing department should design the trade show booth, and trade show materials, reserve the show booth, develop the tactics used before / during / after the trade show, gather the leads and sales data, and calculate the metrics associated with the trade show.

Codes for Sales Team: Think of your sales team as walking brochures for your company. They will convey your image and branding to your prospects and clients. Who they are, how they dress, how they speak, and how they follow up with your clients will control your company brand in the eyes of your customers.

Remember, you need to tell your company story, or someone else will write it for you. Be sure that a few rogue sales people are not writing your company story. Your company image is portrayed through your sales people. Many customers will never meet the other people within the company. They will never tour your offices, review your processes, or understand your customer service policies. The sales person is often the only link that a company has with its clients.

For this reason, the marketing department needs to have some level of oversight into the dress, language, and conduct of the sales team. They do not need to confront the sales team, but rather communicate the brand and image to the sales manager so he or she can maintain the codes and standards. Insurance sales people are known for their dark suits, while landscape professionals are often expected to wear logo polo shirts. Both images are well suited for their business category, but they must be defined in advance through the marketing process.

Be sure that you invest time into understanding how the dress code and conduct of your sales team impacts the final sale. You may find that by altering the current codes, sales will be increased. Would landscape professionals close more sales, or fewer sales, if they wore dark suits? The prospective customers would likely be shocked to see them arrive at their home dressed in this fashion. However, a landscape professional would certainly have more success if they convey a brand that is professional, clean, and reliable. Consider these factors within the sales process and test them, as you would any other marketing tactic.

Sales Meetings: The marketing team should attend sales meetings to better understand the needs and metrics of the sales team. Many terrific ideas will be adopted, and expensive errors avoided, by facilitating open communications between sales and marketing. The marketing department should rely on the sales team, and the sales team should rely on the marketing department. The sales team has critical information to share with marketing. While marketing needs to enforce the corporate branding, sales processes, and metrics, the two departments must work closely together in order to be successful. One of the best ways to develop close ties between the two departments is inviting the marketing people to sales meetings, and including the sales team in marketing meetings.

After reading these first few pages of this chapter, you may be nodding in agreement, feeling sick to your stomach, or laughing at the foolishness of this proposal. Your company culture may be very entrenched, making it impossible to get sales and marketing to work together. On the other hand, your sales manager may already oversee the marketing function and the marketing and sales functions could be closely entwined. Both approaches are common within a business.

It is not my goal to create conflict within your company. Rather, the approach of this book is centered on formula marketing. If you want your company to be successful, to reach the next level, and to develop a marketing formula that generates profitable results every quarter, you need to closely align your sales and marketing departments.

It is imperative that marketing understands and supports the sales process. How else can marketing select the best lead sources, design programs to generate those leads, and the proper tools to assist those leads in the decision making process? Marketing will see things that the sales team will miss. The sales team will have the hands-on experience with the prospect demographics that marketing will use to refine the messaging strategy. The two departments work best when they work together.

Additionally, certain tools and processes need to be implemented to allow marketing to support the sales department. These tools are fundamental to a modern sales department. However, I know many companies that work without them. The list follows:

Company-Wide CRM System: CRM is simply an abbreviation for Customer Relationship Management. There are many terrific CRM tools available today on the market. Programs like SalesForce.com, ACT!, Gold Mine, and PipelineDeals.com provide a centralized database for sales people to maintain their customer database, input notes about their conversations, keep records of their transactions, and post reminders for their follow-up activities.

A CRM system will also allow you to export an up-to-date Excel file or csv file to use as a mailing list or an e-campaign list. While many sales professionals use tools like this in their daily work, it is less common for the entire sales team within a single company to be using the same system. This makes generating a single company-wide database for marketing campaigns a great deal more difficult. Multiple systems also fail to vet duplicates, so two or three sales people could be contacting the same prospect or company.

Additionally, without a centralized CRM, the sales manager does not have adequate control over the current clients and prospects. If the sales person leaves the company, the database will often leave with them. With a centralized CRM, the sales manager can see the activity level of his sales people, witness their productivity, know the strength of the current pipeline, track current quotes and proposals, have the tools to project sales for the month and quarter, and build the important metrics for the entire sales process.

If your sales department does nothing else new, make sure they implement a company-wide, common CRM system. Then be sure to enforce the system's use and maintenance. An out-of-date database is completely worthless to your company. It is critical that the CRM is used daily by each sales professional and maintained by every member of the sales team.

Simplify the Sales Process – for the Sales Team: Some companies have a very simple sales process, while in other companies the selling process involves complicated estimates, detailed proposals, and lengthy state and federal disclosure requirements. There are often many complicated steps required to qualify a buyer, quote the project, approve the sale, manufacture the ordered item, and approve the client's credit or terms. Each of these steps cost money.

The sales process is different for every company and every industry. However, there are always opportunities to simplify the sales process for your sales team and your customers.

During your sales meetings, be sure to review the sales process frequently. Ask for ideas for reducing the number of steps, eliminating or consolidating forms, accelerating the estimating process, and speeding up the credit approvals. All of this time will impact your close ratios. If you are able to quickly quote, approve, close and process a sales order, you will have a higher sales close ratio and a more effective sales team.

Your sales people are often the highest paid employees within your company, so be sure to streamline their workload as much as possible to generate the highest possible ROI. Develop simple systems, or hire specific staff, to support the estimates, proposals, job order forms, and credit approvals. You want your sales people doing what they do best – selling. They should spend as little time as possible filling out forms, completing estimates, attending meetings, and writing proposals. Look at ways to create online template forms, price lists, and e-mail RFQs. Hire sales support staff to offload the paperwork and the customer follow-up tasks so your sales team is focused primarily on new business opportunities.

There are hundreds of ways to simplify the sales process. See if your sales team can create one new time-saving step in each weekly sales meeting. Push through the antiquated systems and the tired "we have always done it this way" objections and continue to create innovations within your processes.

The companies with the most efficient internal systems are more productive, more responsive, and more profitable. Capitalize on these inexpensive ways to improve your sales productivity and you will receive a solid return on your investment of time and energy. You will also attract and develop better sales people, because they will be speaking with more prospects, scheduling more meetings, giving more webinars, generating more sales, and making more money. The whole organization wins.

Never skimp on your sales force. Hire the best. Pay them well. Do not reduce or eliminate their commissions. Be sure to give them the right tools. And always look for ways to simplify the selling process. If you do these things consistently, you will have a very productive and profitable sales department.

Simplify the Sales Process – for the Customer: I often marvel at how many sales are lost, or nearly lost, because the sales process is too complicated or slow for the customer. The core of sales should be making the qualification, quoting, and closing process as easy for the consumer as possible. It should be your sales manager's obsession to remove obstacles for the customer's dollars to flow quickly into the company.

If you want to attract and retain customers, make it as easy for them as possible to buy from you. Your customers want a high quality product or service at a fair price that takes them very little time and makes their life easier. Be sure that every step of the sales process encourages this experience and reinforces these concepts. If you fail in this area, you will quite simply lose customers to your competition.

It is critical that you remove all obstacles to the customer. Here is a list of things that you can do to simplify the sales process for your customers:

- Include easy-to-understand **Directions** within all of your advertising

- **Offers** that are Easy to Understand
- **Signage** that is prominently displayed and easy to read
- Plenty of **Parking**
- **Fast**, reliable service (Remember Surf Brother Teriyaki serves every meal in less than a minute)
- **Friendly** and knowledgeable customer service
- Provide the customer with a clear explanation of **What** they are buying
- Provide the customer with a clear schedule of **When** the item will be completed
- **Eliminate** unnecessary forms
- **Reduce** the size and complexity of forms
- Provide fast **estimates** and quotes
- Develop easy to understand **prices** and price lists
- Explain the **options** (like upgrades and warranties) clearly and limit them to just a few
- Make the items easy to **reach, carry**, and **place** in their car
- Make the solutions easy to **implement**
- If they have to wait, give them something **interesting** to do
- Provide thorough **training** when necessary
- Give around-the-clock **support**, **online tools**, and **people** to contact if they have an issue

You get the idea.

One of the keys to successful sales and customer retention is to make the customer's experience with your company as easy as possible. Save them time, eliminate their worry, reduce their stress, make them look like a hero, and reduce their liabilities.

If there are complicated steps that cannot be avoided in the selling process, make sure you take care of these items for your customer. Make it easy for them and difficult for your company. This is a terrific customer service opportunity. Clearly explain the need for each step of the sales process and then tell your customer "Your time is important, so we will take care of this for you". Adopting this simple concept will help you attract and retain more customers.

I know these are common sense concepts. However, I witness hundreds of examples each week of companies that make it difficult for customers to buy their products or spend their money. Imagine the improved cash flow and profits if each of these companies invested time and energy to unlock ways to allow their customers to give them their money more quickly.

Simple is not always simple. It often takes a great deal of hard work to make something simple. However, the investment to simplify your sales process will pay steady dividends.

Create a Sales Formula: We have covered formula marketing for several chapters. I hope that I have made a compelling case for the value of creating marketing formulas that generate improved and more predictable results. The same opportunities exist with sales. It is possible to develop a highly effective sales formula.

Your sales formula can involve lead generation, lead qualification, corporate messaging, a simplified sales process, closing techniques, customer service, after-sale strategies, and referral programs. Rather than "selling by the seat of your pants", develop consistent, proven steps to your selling process, and track your metrics for each important step. Understand your sales ratios, like lead generation, qualification, close ratios, number of days to close a sale, cost per lead, and cost per sale.

We have covered these concepts throughout the book, so by now you recognize the application of formula marketing to the creation of a sales formula. The concepts are interchangeable with your sales processes. In fact, formulas can be implemented for virtually every aspect of successful living.

People use formulas with their finances. They use them in their health, diet and exercise programs. People use formulas in their sports, hobbies, housework, and daily activities. Many people even use a formulaic approach to their prayer life. Why? Simply because formulas work.

A good formula will distill the important elements of any activity into a series of proven steps. Formulas are most helpful to the novice, but they are also used by the master in virtually every discipline. Formulas accelerate results, improve ratios for success, and simplify the processes needed to complete a task effectively. Therefore, to achieve success in business, Formula Marketing is more than a good idea. It is a proven approach.

For additional ideas and support, I invite you to visit our website at www.formula-marketing.com. I am also available to provide a workshop or direct consulting to your business group or company.

It is my hope that you will implement Formula Marketing within your business. I hope that the ideas and concepts shared with you in this book will help you to achieve your goals and objectives. This book will conclude with three, final examples of Formula Marketing to illustrate how to develop a successful formula for your business. I can think of no better way to summarize the content of Formula Marketing. Thank you for your investment of time and money in reading this book. I want to wish you great success in your business endeavors with Formula Marketing.

CHAPTER 16:
FORMULA MARKETING SUMMARY –
EXAMPLE ONE

CleanTech: High-Tech Company with annual sales of $15 million

Formula Marketing: CleanTech, Inc.

Description: A small, hi-tech company based in Boulder, CO, CleanTech manufacturers and sells a line of clean room products used by many high-tech companies in their prototype and production manufacturing. CleanTech manufactures equipment designed for a wide variety of clean room environments. They have a strong presence in the semiconductor, microwave, and data storage industries. They have been in business for fifteen years and have a staff of 40 people. They use contract manufacturers to produce their products, but handle all of the design and engineering from their Boulder office. They have a staff of five sales people who cover the United States, and a network of distributors that handles their sales in Asia and Europe.

Step 1: Authority and Expectations: Steve Wilson holds the position of Director of Marketing of CleanTech and reports directly to the company president. He works closely with the Director of Sales and the Director of Customer Service to understand the needs of his customers and the needs of his sales team. Steve has complete control of his annual marketing budget of $450,000, which is 3% of annual corporate revenue of $15,000,000. Steve works with the executive team to develop corporate objectives, and then creates and executes the CleanTech marketing plan to achieve those objectives.

Step 2: Marketing Metrics: Steve has developed a series of metrics that allow him to track the success of his marketing programs. He actively tracks the following metrics:

Marketing Tactic And Resulting Metrics:

Website: Number of Hits
CleanTech Weekly Blog: Open Rate / Number of Click-Thrus
E-Campaigns: Open Rate / Number of Click-Thrus
Field Demonstrations: RSVPs / Attendance / Leads / Sales
Internet Advertising: Landing Page Hits / # of Leads / Sales Tracked to Advertising
Direct Mail: Number of Calls / Landing Page Hits / Special Offers Redeemed
Tradeshows: Number of Leads / Visits to Booth / Appointments Scheduled / Sales
Trade Publication Advertising: Calls / Landing Page Hits / Special Offers Redeemed

Step 3: Define Your Customer:

CleanTech sells directly to procurement managers, buyers, R&D engineering teams and production engineering teams. They sell primarily to the semiconductor, data storage, and microwave industries. Their customer list is comprised of 200 large high-tech manufacturing companies and 300 smaller companies that directly serve those major manufacturers. These 500 companies are based in the United States. Their distributors in Asia and Europe sell directly to the same company groups in those country regions, with approximately 800 customer companies in Asia and 60 customer companies in Europe. Currently, 70% of sales come from the United States, 22% from Asia, and 8% from Europe.

Step 4: Differentiate Your Business:

CleanTech is an engineering company. They have developed a reputation for solving tough engineering problems within prototype and production manufacturing for their core industries. Their team of experts are known for their production engineering expertise. All of their engineers have extensive experience and contacts within the semiconductor, microwave, and data storage industries where they have served as top production engineers. No other company within their industry has a team of engineers with the direct knowledge and experience of the CleanTech team. While the engineering team develops and maintains the product line, they also interface actively with the customer base, assist with equipment implementation, training and support. CleanTech carries a higher price then most of their competitors. Their value proposition is focused on saving their customers time and money by helping them to develop high-yield, low issue production environments using CleanTech products.

Step 5: Write your Marketing Plan:

I. Situational Analysis: Condensed

CleanTech has eight major competitors. Three of the competitors are based in the United States, and five are based in other countries, with offices in the United States that support their sales and customer service functions. The Situational Analysis for CleanTech includes a complete profile of each of these competitor companies, including their product lines, prices, people, advertising, and operations. The Situational Analysis keeps a record of all of the available industry tradeshows, advertising vehicles, and industry events.

The CleanTech Situational Analysis also has an in-depth profile of its own company, with complete records of annual sales for the past 10 years, top customers, past advertising and marketing results, sales and profit margins by product, cash position, image within the industry, and the complete details of its product line. The Situational Analysis contains a complete SWOT analysis that discusses CleanTech's strengths, weaknesses, opportunities, and threats. This profile is updated each quarter by Steve Wilson. The profile also includes complete details of the work experience, results, and expertise of the CleanTech engineering, customer service, and sales staff.

The CleanTech Situational Analysis also provides a summary of the current market conditions within each of the major industries they serve. This summary discusses the dominant players within each industry, the best customer prospects, opportunities for growth, new products that are needed, new companies that are emerging, economic conditions, and key industry trends.

II. Objectives:

Each year, Steve Wilson hosts a series of meetings with the entire corporate office team to develop the annual company Objectives. This year, the key Objectives are centered on improving overall sales, increasing profitability, and lowering the cost per lead. This year's list of Objectives follows:

- Increase Annual Sales by $3,000,000 over Previous Year for Total Annual Sales of $18,000,000
  US Sales Objective: Increase sales from $10,500,000 to $12,000,000
  Asian Sales Objective: Increase sales from $3,300,000 to $4,500,000
  European Sales Objective: Increase sales from $1,200,000 to $1,500,000

- Recruit 40 New Clients (at $50,000 average sales this year) = $2,000,000

- Retain All Current Clients (Total: 175) from Previous Year

- Increase Total Sales to Current Clients by $1,000,000 over Previous Year

- Increase Average Annual Client Spend from $85,000 to $92,000

- Lower Cost per Lead from $4,500 to $2,250 this year

- Lower Cost per New Customer from $23,000 to $11,000

- Increase Average Sales per Sales Team Member from $2,100,000 to $2,400,000

- Increase Annual Gross Profit from $3,000,000 to $4,500,000

III. Strategies:

To attain these Objectives, Steve and the executive team developed the following series of Strategies:

- Recruit 40 New Customers by Targeting the Key Clients of our Top Competitors, using Experienced Engineering and Improved Production Thru-Put as our core Value Proposition.

- Increase Average Sales by Sales Representatives with Improved Engineering Support. Create 15% more time for Engineering Staff by Outsourcing Project Scheduling Tasks.

- Improve Profit Margins and Increase Average Client Spend by Up-Selling expanded Engineering Consulting Services with Comprehensive Product Implementation Programs.

- Retain All Clients with Comprehensive Customer Support Campaign Focused on Solving Customer's "Top 3 Issues" through expanded Engineering Consulting Program.

- Improve Each Customer's Experience with CleanTech by speeding up Product Delivery and Implementation through increased productivity of engineering staff, improved scheduling capabilities, and JIT inventory programs with key suppliers.

- Improve Cost Per Lead and Cost per New Client by reducing presence in European Tradeshows, Negotiating Better Advertising Rates in Key Publications, and Developing Three Cost and Lead Sharing Strategic Corporate Partnerships.

VI. Tactics:

With the company Objectives and Strategies in hand, Steve wrote a Classic 5 Step Marketing Plan for the new year, where he revised CleanTech's Situational Analysis, detailed the new corporate Objectives and put the new Strategies into words. With these first three steps in place,

Steve developed the Tactics for the year in Step 4, using his proven Marketing Matrix to select his leading tactics. The CleanTech tactics follow:

Tactic One: Identify 10 Potential Strategic Partners. Rank in order of Best Potential. Develop Strategic Partnership Presentation and Agreements. Develop "Deadline Strategy" for quick decisions by target Strategic Partners based on Advertising Contract and Tradeshow Deadline Dates. "Close" top Three Strategic Partners.
Budget: $5,000   **Completion Date:** December 1st

Tactic Two: Purchase and assign a series of call tracking numbers for each specific tactic, publication, and marketing activity so each can be accurately tracked.
Budget: $1,800   **Completion Date:** September 15th

Tactic Three: Negotiate New Annual Contract with TechPress, which controls two of the three key Trade Publications for the semiconductor and data storage industries. Request additional 25% discount for full-page ads in both publications for the entire year. This contract to include the insertion of coded CleanTech promotional flyer in two issues, prior to two major trade shows (see **Tactic Four**). Use the TechPress contract as leverage to negotiate the same 25% discount and coded flyer insertion provision in an annual contract with Anderson Trades, the owner of the third publication.
Budget: $200,000   **Completion Date:** November 5th

Tactic Four: Develop new Ad Campaign focused on Experienced Engineering and Higher Thru-Put. The campaign will feature a profile series that focuses on the specific experience of each member of the CleanTech engineering team. Use this campaign in trade publication advertising, direct mail campaigns, inserts, tradeshow collateral, and website. Integrate mentions and corporate logos of Strategic Partners in the new campaign creative.
Budget: $15,000   **Completion Date:** November 30th

Tactic Five: Design and implement a 12-Part, 20,000-piece Direct Mail Campaign for the existing customer list and new target database with landing pages, call tracking number, and e-newsletter opt-in that includes the new experienced engineering and higher thru-put campaign. Include a "Free Engineering Consulting Package", "Free Product Upgrades" and other special offers and calls-to-action to track the direct mail response rates. Develop 6 different versions of the offer to test the best performer. Each offer will be coded, so the results of each specific offer can be tracked. When printing the 65,000 direct mail pieces, overprint by 70,000 for use as inserts in trade publications, tradeshow flyers, and tradeshow bag stuffers, for a total "gang" print run of 135,000 pieces. Each of these pieces will be coded by type, so CleanTech can track the results of each piece. The native files will be provided to European and Asian distributors to create their own campaigns. This print run is for US operations only. A summary follows:

Printed Version and Quantity of Pieces:
- **Direct Mail Campaign to Existing Customers**

  CleanTech has 175 current customers with an average of 10 contacts within each customer company, for a total of 1,750 current customer contacts. Additional pieces are added for new customers that are added to the database during the year.

  12 Mailings = 12 versions with 6 different offers: 25,000 pieces

- **Direct Mail Campaign to Target Non-Customers**

  CleanTech has 325 non-customers with an average of 10 target contacts within each customer company, for a total of 3,250 non-customer contacts.

  12 Mailings = 12 versions with 6 different offers: 40,000 pieces

- **Trade Publication Inserts**

  CleanTech will insert these pieces into 3 publications, two times each, for a total of 6 insertions. The total monthly circulation of all three publications is 25,000.

  Total of 6 Insertions @ 1 version each = 6 versions: 50,000 pieces

- **Trade Show Flyers / Trade Show Bag Stuffers**

CleanTech will attend 8 tradeshows in the US and will use a different flyer version for each tradeshow, so the results can be tracked.

  8 Trade Shows = 8 versions with same offer: 20,000 pieces

  Total Versions: 38

  Total Pieces: 135,000

  Total Budget (includes printing, mail services, and postage): $ 45,000

  Completion Date: December 15th

Tactic Six: Send monthly E-Newsletter / E-Campaign to customer database e-mails. Design and implement an on-line template so the monthly content can be added quickly and easily. Develop a calendar of articles and features on "Experienced Engineering" and include case studies of "Higher Thru-Put" using actual customer experiences. Open rates, click-thrus and links to a special landing page will track responses. Monthly E-mails can be sent at no charge, template creation is the only cost.

Budget: $2,500   **Completion Date:** December 15th

Tactic Seven: Revise Website to include new "Experienced Engineering" and "Higher-Thru-Put" Campaign. Add 15 landing pages (3 for the 3 trade publications, 8 for the 8 trade shows,

1 for the existing customer direct mail campaign, 1 for the non-customer direct mail campaign, 1 for all Internet advertising, and 1 for the e-Newsletter). Build each landing page with the required metadata and key words to boost SEO rankings. Link to monthly Blogs.

Budget: $5,000   **Completion Date:** January 5th

Tactic Eight: Develop a series of press releases for local newspapers, online press, trade publications focused on "Experienced Engineering" and recent client product launches with CleanTech support. Develop and print a comprehensive Press Kit with company history, facts, current photos, CEO travel schedule, and story ideas. Use e-Public Relations to proliferate the press releases throughout the Internet and boost CleanTech's SEO ranking. Press releases to be written in-house and posted to "News" page on website. Write a monthly Blog with industry updates, advancements, and observations. Post Blog to website.

New Corporate Photography: $2,000
Print and Mail 500 Press Kits: $3,000
Hire e-PR Company for Press Release Distribution: $15,000
Total Budget: $20,000   **Completion Date:** January 15 – December 5

Tactic Nine: Attend 8 United States Trade Shows. Reserve booth locations, reserve trade show booth for each event; schedule staff for each show; purchase promotional items, trade show bags (with direct mail pieces inserted) and candy. Print and mail trade show invitations to current customer list and non-customer list for each show and include booth location. Print and mail follow-up pieces; post trade show schedule on website. Schedule CEO's travel around trade shows, so he is available for key meetings at the shows.

Promotional Items: $4,500
Air Travel: $25,000
Hotel: $10,000
Meals: $ 8,500
Tradeshow Booths: $45,000
Booth Shipping and Set-Up: $15,000
Print and Mail Trade Show Invitations: $10,000
Print and Mail Trade Show Follow-up Pieces: $2,500
Total Budget: $120,500   **Completion Date:** October 20th

Tactic Ten: Attend 4 Asian Trade Shows to support distributors. Combine trade shows with visits to key Asian customers and on-site demonstrations. Coordinate travel plans with key distributors. Trade show expenses to be covered by distributors. Staff travel to be covered by CleanTech.

Budget: $15,000   **Completion Date:** February - October

Tactic Eleven: Develop on-site demonstration schedule that is coordinated with sales and engineering product implementation visits. Travel and expenses to be covered under "cost of goods sold" within client's purchase orders. Invite non-competing customers within region to visit and witness new product implementation and higher thru-put examples. Invite new strategic partners. Leverage sales team and sales budget to cover all additional costs.
Budget: $0   **Completion Date:** January - December

Tactic Twelve: Develop Case Studies from Current Customers that illustrate "Experienced Engineering" and "Higher Thru-Put". Add Case Studies to e-Newsletter, website, design and print 10,000 copies of 4-page Case Study Kit for Trade Show Hand-outs, and use in Press Releases.
Budget: $4,000   **Completion Date:** November 30

Tactic Thirteen: As part of "Experienced Engineering Campaign", an engineer will accompany sales team on every important sales call to support sales, product implementation and customer service. Provide travel schedule of top engineers to local papers for interviews and to strategic partners for key meetings. Leverage sales budget to cover costs of the program.
Budget: $0   **Completion Date:** January - December

Tactic Fourteen: Purchase banner ads on the websites of publications and key industry trade associations. Leverage strategic partnerships to cover the costs and cross-promote each other's products on websites and landing pages.
Budget: $10,000   **Completion Date:** January 15th

Total "Actual" Marketing Budget: $443,800
Total "Reserved" Marketing Budget: $450,000

V. Assessment:
Steve Wilson will assess the success and results of each of the marketing strategies and tactics by compiling the metrics needed to see if he has accomplished CleanTech's company objectives. As part of this effort, Steve will use his corporate metrics, sales reports and accounting reports to track the following:

- Total Company Sales: US Sales / Asian Sales / European Sales
- Number of New Clients Recruited / Number of Current Clients Retained
- Total Sales by Current Clients / Average Annual Client Spend
- Number of Leads Generated and Cost per Lead
- Number of New Customers and Cost per New Customer

- Average Sales per Sales Team Member
- Annual Gross Profit

Marketing Dashboard: Steve Wilson will develop a marketing dashboard to graphically illustrate and track the success of his campaigns, the key metrics, and the data that will be used in his assessment.

Optimizing your Marketing Matrix: CleanTech currently has a marketing matrix that includes 5 key tactics: (1) US Trade Shows, (2) Trade Publications, (3) Public Relations, (4) Direct Mail, and (5) Website / Internet Marketing.

Steve is testing the following new programs: (1) Strategic Partnerships, (2) e-Newsletters, (3) Case Studies, (4) New Campaign focused on "Experienced Engineering" and "Higher Thru-Put, (5) On-Site Demonstrations, (6) Attending Asian Trade Shows and (7) Invitations and Follow-up pieces for US Trade Shows. He will carefully evaluate his results compared with last year, and track the important metrics to determine which of these new tactics will remain.

Corporate Brand: Steve will develop the new campaign, "Experienced Engineering and Higher-Thru-Put", around his current logo and brand. He will use consistent messaging, images, design, and colors throughout his direct mail, tradeshows, banner ads, website, e-Newsletters, and other tactics.

Additional Items: Steve will negotiate his buys carefully and will leverage his strategic partnerships to lower costs for trade publication advertising, public relations, Internet advertising, collateral, tradeshows, promotional items, and website development.

Steve Wilson has used Formula Marketing effectively to design his marketing plan to attain CleanTech's corporate objectives. While every tactic may not succeed, Steve will have the ability to track all of his results and quickly determine what changes he needs to make for the next year. In summary, Steve Wilson will know if his marketing formula was a success and why. Over time, he will build a formula that works and generates reliable, predictable results. His marketing expenditures will reflect carefully planned investments, rather than a series of random expenses. He will have a proven marketing formula.

CHAPTER 17:
FORMULA MARKETING SUMMARY –
EXAMPLE TWO

Bailey Builders: Home Remodeling Company with annual sales of $12 million

Formula Marketing: Bailey Builders, Inc.

Description: Bailey Builders is a family-owned, home remodeling company based in Seattle, WA. Bailey Builders specializes in room additions, whole house renovations, kitchen and bath remodeling projects, and second-story additions. They have a reputation for quality in the Seattle community. They have been in business for thirty-two years, have won several local building awards, have been recognized by the Better Business Bureau as one of Seattle's best remodeling companies, and have a staff of 35 people. They act as general contractors, employ an in-house architect in order to offer design services, and work closely with a team of carefully selected, high-quality subcontractors for the specific tasks required for each project.

Step 1: Authority and Expectations: Jennifer Bailey serves as Bailey Builders' Marketing Manager. She reports directly to her uncle, the president of Bailey Builders. A recent graduate of business school, Jennifer is eager to build a brand for Bailey Builders. Jennifer works closely with the project managers, who handle the project bids and direct sales. Jennifer is working hard to establish her credentials as a marketing professional, with an eye toward running the company one day. With persistence, she has carved out an annual marketing budget of $200,000, which is just over 1.5% of annual sales of $12,000,000. This is the first time in company history that Bailey Builders has had a formal marketing budget. Jennifer negotiated complete autonomy over the marketing budget. With that control, Jennifer decided to work closely with the entire company and build consensus for each of the marketing tactics. She determined the corporate objectives and strategies and presented them to the entire company just before the annual picnic. The staff was both impressed and excited by her plans and enthusiasm.

Step 2: Marketing Metrics: Jennifer began by creating a series of metrics that she would need to track the success of her marketing initiatives.

Marketing Tactic And Resulting Metrics:

Home & Garden Shows: Booth Visits / Leads / Sales
Direct Mail Campaigns: Calls / Leads / Offers Redeemed - Sales
E-Campaigns: Open Rate / Number of Click-Thrus
Open Houses for Completed Projects: RSVPs / Attendance / Leads / Sales
Internet Advertising: Landing Page Hits / # of Leads / Sales Tracked to Advertising
Yellow Page Advertising: Calls / Leads / Sales / Website Visits
Radio Advertising – Saturday Morning Program: Calls / Leads / Landing Page Hits / Sales Tracked to Radio
Strategic Partnerships & Networking Groups: Leads / Click-Thurs to Landing Page Hits / Sales from Each Strategic Partner

Step 3: Define Your Customer:

Bailey Builders has a reputation for quality. They do things right the first time. They work with very experienced subcontractors. As a result, their services are priced higher than most of their competitors. Their customers have high levels of income, high net worth, and live in the wealthier communities of Seattle. They do not have a formal customer list yet, but a series of records for each of the projects they have done in the past, along with before and after photos from each project. Bailey Builders will only take projects valued at over $100,000.

Step 4: Differentiate Your Business:

Bailey Builders builds close relationships with its customers. Most of their projects will span 6 to 12 months. Over the course of each project, they form close friendships with many of their clients, as they are in their homes every day for several hours. Additionally, they are very supportive within the architectural design process. They handle all of the design approvals, permits, and required certificates. Bailey Builders is famous for completing their projects on-schedule and on-budget. Their key differentiator is the quality of their workmanship. They have a reputation for being the highest quality home remodel company in Seattle.

Step 5: Write your Marketing Plan:

I. Situational Analysis: Condensed

Bailey Builders competes with hundreds of home remodeling companies and general contractors. However, only three other companies in Seattle share a similar reputation for quality, work exclusively for the wealthiest home owners, have the same level of customer service, and attention to detail, and offer the complete design capabilities. Bailey Builders frequently submits proposals alongside these three other companies. These other three companies have large marketing budgets, advertise consistently, and have annual sales at least twice those of Bailey Builders.

Jennifer Bailey is writing her first Situational Analysis. She is now tracking the advertising activities of each of these three competitors. She visits their booths at the home show, keeps copies of all of their print advertising, and tracks their radio and television advertising. Jennifer tracks every project that Bailey Builders loses to one of these companies. She follows up with the homeowners once the project is complete to survey their experiences and asks specific questions of how these companies do in relation to completing the project on-schedule, on-budget, and the satisfaction of the homeowner. Additionally, Jennifer has started to interview her clients at the conclusion of every project. She provides them with a formal questionnaire, and then sits down with them to review their answers. Her open-ended discussion will bring out additional details that the survey did not cover. Jennifer provides each client with a gift to thank them for their business and their time in completing the survey and project completion interview. She then catalogs all of her findings and survey results, and compares the satisfaction ratings with those of her three top competitors.

The state of the local economy has a significant impact on the home construction and remodeling business. Recessions have a direct and profound impact on industry activity levels and sales. Conversely, when the housing industry is hot, Bailey Builders has a project calendar booked several months in advance. Fortunately, the Seattle economy, based largely on locally-based high-technology firms, often leads the nation. Bailey Builders works with many of the top executives and owners of these firms. Additionally, Bailey Builders has a very good reputation in the medical and legal communities and handles the project needs of many of Seattle's top lawyers and physicians. The Bailey Builders client is more resilient and less price sensitive during times of recession.

Jennifer Bailey's Situational Analysis will begin to summarize the current market conditions within Seattle. It will track the major moves of Seattle's largest high-tech firms and follow the promotions of their key executives. Her Situational Analysis will track the costs of building materials, track the estimates of her subcontractors, and track the projects they win vs. the projects they lose. The Situational Analysis will also watch new players within the industry, study local and national design and building trends, and track the interest rates and lending trends of the local banking community.

By studying their accounting and sales records for the past five years, Jennifer learned the following about Bailey Builders:

- Bailey Builders wins 32% of their project proposals.
- Average cost of a Bailey Builders project is $345,000.

- Average length of a project is 7 months.
- 74% of their business came from client referrals.
- The average sales cycle to win a project is 3.5 months.

Jennifer used the accounting records to build a database of past clients. She then hired a mailing list company to profile her client list, to determine who these customers were, where they lived, the value of their homes, and their income levels. This is what she learned:

- 87% of their client projects were located within 4 zip codes, with 9 other zip codes making up the balance.
- The average, current home value for each client is $765,000.
- The average household income of a Bailey Builders client is $225,000.
- Average Age of a Bailey Builder client: 54
- Average Length of Home Ownership: 9 years
- The Bailey Builders client profile includes: professionals (lawyers, doctors, accountants), top executives, business owners
- 79% have a college degree, and 31% have a graduate degree or higher.
- Bailey Builders clients fall into three major "family" categories:
  Married Couples with Children: 34%
  Married Couples / Recent Empty Nesters: 42%
  Married Couples / Active Retired: 18%

II. Objectives:

As mentioned previously, Jennifer Bailey presented the corporate Objectives at the annual company picnic. The key Objectives are focused on generating more leads, increasing the number of building projects, increasing company sales, and building the company brand. Jennifer realizes that it will take time to move the needle at Bailey Builders, so she has set objectives that will require three years to attain. She has established incremental objectives for each of the next three years, allowing Bailey Builders to reach the following Objectives:

- Increase Annual Sales from $12,000,000 to $20,000,000 in three years
- Generate an average of 400 new "qualified" sales leads per year
- Maintain proposal win ratio of 32%
- Maintain average project cost of $350,000
- Increase annual number of project bids from 115 to 200
- Increase number of new projects from 37 to 65 in three years
- Build a recognized and respected brand for Bailey Builders

III. Strategies:

To attain these Objectives, Jennifer developed the following Strategies. She created her Strategies in a way that discusses some of the related Tactics so the entire company would understand this portion of her plan:

- Generate 400 New "Qualified" Customer Leads and 200 new Project Bids each year by targeting the most affluent homeowners in Seattle through advertising, direct mail, home shows, and radio, focused (when possible) on the four zip codes that have historically brought us most of our sales.

- Increase leads and bid opportunities through a comprehensive customer referral program to our past and existing customers.

- Maintain our proposal win ratio of 32% by developing a professional, comprehensive sales presentation that focuses on the Bailey Builder's 5-Steps to Success: (1) Listen Carefully to Needs and Wants of the Customer, (2) Make Dreams Come True Through Better Design, (3) Solve Building Issues with Experience, (4) Finish On-Schedule and On-Budget by using the Best Subcontractors in their Areas of Expertise, and (5) Require Daily Communication with Everyone using the Bailey Builders Online Schedule Notes Program (this shared document program was developed by one of the Bailey Builders project managers to allow everyone involved with a project to see the progress notes and plan revisions). A project manager must be involved in every sales presentation.

- Bailey Builders will continue to only take projects valued at over $100,000. We will qualify projects in advance of a meeting by asking three questions: (1) Can you please tell me about your project?, (2) What is your budget for this project?, and (3) When would you like to start your project? Once these questions are answered, the appointment will be scheduled.

- Establish the Bailey brand for quality by developing consistent marketing collateral materials, hosting a series of "Open Houses", and hosting a Saturday Morning Radio Show that instructs homeowners and contractors on home remodeling.

VI. Tactics:

Jennifer shared the company Objectives and Strategies with the entire company at the company picnic. She then passed out specially printed Bailey Builders note pads to everyone in the company, including spouses and children. The note pads had Jennifer's Objectives and Strategies printed on the first page, followed by 50 blank pages for their ideas. She explained that the current Objectives and Strategies were just starting points, and that nothing had been decided yet.

After her brief presentation, she asked everyone to go off on their own for 20 minutes to write down their ideas for accomplishing the Objectives and Strategies for Bailey Builders on the pads. When they came back, she put everyone into 5 teams to discuss their ideas. Leaders within the teams were selected randomly. Each leader wrote down the best ideas on a poster board. Then each of the teams took turns sharing their ideas with the whole group. Jennifer saved all of the notes from everyone's pad sheets, as well as the ideas that made it to the posters. The employees were asked to keep the pads with them when they worked, so they could write down new ideas, and share them with the team.

By involving the entire company in the process of developing the Tactics, Jennifer allowed everyone to have a voice in the marketing plan. She realized that she was new to a marketing leadership role and wanted to include everyone in the creative process, rather than try to "prove" herself. Her method produced the following Tactics:

Tactic One: Develop a Direct Mail campaign focused on "Quality Craftsmen" that targets the most affluent homeowners within the 4 zip codes that have brought Bailey Builders the most projects. We will only mail to homes that have a value of $500,000 or higher, and income levels of $150,000 and higher. The campaign will focus on quality remodeling and will include photographs of completed projects, with testimonials from our clients. We will feature our guarantee that every project will be completed on-schedule and on-budget. We will also feature our building awards and provide an insert with an invitation to tune in to our Saturday Morning Radio Show. We will over-print the direct mail pieces to use at home design shows. We will use call tracking numbers, landing pages and a series of special offers to track results.

Budget: $29,500   **Completion Date:** February 15th

The Specifics of the Tactic One Budget Follow:

Photographs and Graphic Design	$ 3,500
Thank-You Gifts for Testimonials	$ 500
Direct Mail List of 10,000 Homes:	$ 375
Printing of 50,000 Direct Mail Pieces:	$11,500
Printing of 100,000 "Radio Show" Inserts*:	$ 1,250
Mailing Services for 4 Mailings:	$ 1,200
Postage for 4 Mailings X 10,000 Homes:	$10,800
Total Budget:	**$29,125**

Note: 10,000 extra "Radio Show" inserts and direct mail pieces will be used for Home Shows. The 50,000 additional "Radio Show" inserts will be used as magazine inserts.

Tactic Two: Host a Saturday Morning Radio Show on local AM station called "The Quality Craftsmen", focused on offering home remodeling ideas. Use the show to showcase experience as a home remodel expert, generate leads, and build the Bailey Builders brand. Work with current subcontractors to underwrite 50% of the cost of the show. Use call tracking numbers and landing pages to track listening audience, leads, and sales that result from the show. Promote the show through all other forms of marketing, including business cards, invoices, letterhead, brochures, direct mail pieces, and website. Receive additional radio mentions, promotions, and advertisements from radio station as part of sponsorship.

Budget: $62,500   **Completion Date:** November 30th

Tactic Three: Develop customer referral program where current and past customers will receive compensation (weekend vacations, dinners for two, and remodeling discounts) when they refer their friends and neighbors to Bailey Builders. Small gifts will be provided as a "thank-you" for each qualified referral (Ex. Starbucks gift card), while large gifts will be provided when the referred client signs an agreement to complete a project (Ex. dinner for two, Las Vegas weekend, remodel discounts for current projects).

Graphic Design: $ 350
Printing of Referral Brochure: $ 850
Gifts & Discounts: $5,000
Total Budget: $6,200   **Completion Date:** January 15th

Tactic Four: Host "Open Houses" at the completion of each new project. Invite the neighborhood to a cocktail party and tour of the project. Feature "before and after" photographs. Have a local winery provide samples of its latest vintage, local musicians promote their talents, and local restaurants cater the event. These contributions of music, wine and food will be at the expense of these strategic partners. Bailey Builders will cover the costs of the invitations, incidentals, the photographs (which will be provided as gifts to the home owner / client) and other miscellaneous items. A total of 10 "Open Houses" will be offered, based on the willingness of the home owner / client. Attendance, leads and sales will be tracked via RSVPs and sign-in sheets.

Budget: $20,000   **Completion Date:** January - November

Tactic Five: Attend a total of 6 Home and Garden Shows in the Seattle area. Reserve the tradeshow space, design and build the booth using project manager talents, use direct mail pieces as marketing collateral. Staff the booth with several staff members. Design a system for recording all leads for "qualified" prospects that visit the booth (by asking the three questions: (1) Can you please tell me about your project?, (2) What is your budget for this project?, and (3) When would you like to start your project?) Send a "Thank-You" card to every qualified prospect that visits the booth and follow up with a phone offer to provide a free on-site estimate. Attendance at Home Shows will be promoted on Radio Show and mentions of each Home

Show will reduce the cost of the booth rentals by 50%, as part of negotiations with the home show host companies.

Promotional Items: $ 2,500
Collateral: Covered in Direct Mail Expense
Trade Show Booths: $ 7,500
Staffing: $10,000
Booth Materials and Set-Up: $ 5,000
Total Budget: **$25,000**
Completion Date: Per Home Show Schedule

Tactic Six: Develop new sales presentation using video clips, PowerPoint, and portfolio story boards showing actual project phases, concluding with testimonials. Presentations will be given in client homes via laptop with projector and portable portfolio kits.
Budget: $2,500   **Completion Date:** February 15th

Tactic Seven: Refresh website to include new customer testimonials, landing pages for tracking results from direct mail campaign and magazine advertising, and include new project calculator feature. Include new customer testimonials, projects, and update capabilities page. Include keywords within each landing page to boost SEO.
Budget: $3,500   **Completion Date:** January 5th

Tactic Eight: Write Press Releases for local newspapers and magazines focused on Green building trends. Stories to include separate "green web page" to track website visits. Press releases to be written in-house and posted to "News" page on website.
Budget: $0   **Completion Date:** January 1 – December 31

Tactic Nine: Advertise in *Seattle Magazine, Seattle Home* and *Designer's Corner.* Negotiate annual rates with each and include direct mail pieces as inserts as part of the buy. Be sure to mention Radio Show in the display ads and use recent project photographs. Special call tracking numbers and landing pages will track leads and sales.
Budget: $45,000   **Completion Date:** December 1st

Tactic Ten: As the marketing plan is implemented, conduct a series of quarterly mall intercept interviews at high-end malls near the 4 key zip codes to determine brand recognition and rating for the Bailey Builders brand. The questions (3) and number of respondents per survey (500) will not vary, to determine increases in consumer recognition and rating of Bailey Builders brand. Direct mail pieces will be handed to each respondent and they will be asked if they have a project planned within the next 12 months in an effort to generate additional sales leads.
Budget: $850   **Completion Date:** Quarterly

Total "Allocated" Marketing Budget: $195,050
Total Marketing Budget: $200,000

V. Assessment:

Jennifer Bailey will assess the results and success of the marketing strategies and tactics by tracking and studying the metrics to see if she has reached their company objectives. Jennifer will study her corporate metrics, sales reports and accounting reports to track the following:

- Total Company Sales
- Number of Qualified Leads Generated and Cost per Lead
- Most Successful Offers, based on Redemption of Each
- Number of Projects and Cost Per Sold Project
- Number of Project Bids
- Ratio of Projects Won vs. Number of Project Bids
- Total Sales and Project Win Ratio by Each Project Manager
- Average Project Cost
- Annual Gross Profit
- Mall Intercept Interviews to Survey Core Demographic to determine if Bailey Builders has a recognized and respected brand

Marketing Dashboard: Jennifer Bailey will develop a marketing dashboard to track the success of her campaigns and graphically illustrate the key metrics, and the data that will be used in her assessment.

Optimizing your Marketing Matrix: Within their marketing plan, Bailey Builders has a marketing matrix that includes four key tactics: (1) Home Shows, (2) Radio Show, (3) Direct Mail, and (4) Magazine Advertising.

Jennifer will be testing the following new programs: (1) Open Houses, (2) Customer Referral Program, (3) Revised Website and Project Calculator, (4) Public Relations, (5) New Sales Presentation, (5) New "Quality Craftsmen" Campaign, (6) Mall Intercept Interviews, and (7) Special Offers. She will carefully evaluate her results compared with last year, and track the important metrics to determine which of these new tactics will remain.

Corporate Brand: Jennifer will develop the new "Quality Craftsmen" campaign around her current logo and brand. She will use consistent messaging, images, design, and colors throughout her direct mail, home shows, open houses, radio show, and magazine ads.

Additional Items: Jennifer will negotiate her magazine advertising buys carefully and will leverage her radio show to lower her home show costs.

Jennifer Bailey has used Formula Marketing effectively to design her marketing plan to attain Bailey Builders' corporate objectives. While every tactic may not succeed, Jennifer will have the ability to track all of her results and quickly determine what changes are needed to improve her marketing plan for next year. In summary, Jennifer Bailey will know if her marketing formula was a success and why. Over time, she will build a formula that works and generates reliable, predictable results. Her marketing expenditures will reflect carefully planned investments, rather than a series of random expenses. Jennifer will have a proven marketing formula.

CHAPTER 18:
FORMULA MARKETING SUMMARY –
EXAMPLE THREE

Beans: Coffee House Chain with annual sales of $5.8 million

Formula Marketing: Beans, Inc.

Description: Beans is a Phoenix-based chain of 7 coffee houses located primarily in grocery-anchored shopping centers. Beans, Inc. competes directly with international coffee giant Starbucks, and other national coffee house brands, by selling high-quality coffee, tea, and food items. Beans has a corporate office staff of 5 people, with teams of 10 people that operate each store. They have been in business for twelve years and have recently added three new locations. Annual sales are currently at $5,800,000, with a goal of $7,000,000 (an average of $1 million per location) by year end.

Step 1: Authority and Expectations: Katie Smith holds the position of Marketing and HR Manager for Beans, Inc. Katie reports directly to the company owners, Sean and Silvia Preston. She works closely with the manager of each location to understand the needs of their customers and the needs of each location. Katie has gained complete control of her annual marketing budget of $175,000, which is 3% of annual corporate revenue of $5,800,000. Katie works with the company owners and her store managers to develop corporate objectives, and then creates and executes the Beans marketing plan to achieve those objectives.

Step 2: Marketing Metrics: Katie has developed a series of metrics that allow her to track the success of her marketing programs. She actively tracks the following metrics:

Marketing Tactic and Resulting Metrics

Social Media (Twitter, FaceBook, E-Campaigns): Number of Hits / Fans / Click-thrus / Special Offers Redeemed / Sales

Coffee Club Memberships: Number of Cards Issued / Transaction Amount per Card / % of Total Sales / Cards by Store Location / Relationship to Sales

E-Campaigns to Club Members: Open Rate / Number of Click-Thrus / Offers Redeemed / Results Sales

Bounce-Back Coupon Promotions: Number of Transactions / Sales of Mocha Products / Average Ticket

Mystery Shopper: Employee Performance Rankings

Direct Mail Results: Landing Page Hits / Special Offers / Redeemed / Resulting Sales

Cross-Selling Programs: Average Ticket Per Customer

Sale of Catering Services: Catering Calls / Landing Page Hits / Response Rates / Coupons Redeemed / Resulting Sales

Step 3: Define Your Customer:

Beans serves the public. Each location has its own customer profile and the demographics mirror the neighborhood. Near the Arizona State campus, the clients are college-aged students interested in wireless Internet access and plenty of caffeine. The locations in the suburbs attract local home owners, business professionals, and families on the go. Each location has its own personality, defined by the clientele that live near the location.

Step 4: Differentiate Your Business:

Beans offers an alternative to the long lines and giant chain approach of Starbucks. Their locations are simple, bright, warm, fast and very clean. Their menu is a reflection of the restaurant: bright and simple. They want to cater to everyone by taking the mystery out of ordering a cup of coffee, by offering Large, Medium and Small drink sizes. They offer free wireless Internet access, several plugs to accommodate their clients' lap-tops, ample seating, and soft background music. Their prices and offerings are similar to their competition. However, their locations are larger than the average coffee spot and have plenty of seats available. They offer more service, by bringing your order to your table, after it is ordered at the counter. Beans has a thriving catering business. They will bring your order directly to your office or meeting and take care of all of the details. This portion of their business is new and growing rapidly. Additionally, Beans advertises frequently and offers coupons, while most of their competitors do not.

Step 5: Write your Marketing Plan:

I. Situational Analysis: Condensed

Beans has a competitor on every street corner. They divide their competitive analysis store-by-store. They watch the offerings at giants Starbucks and McDonalds very carefully. Beans has its fingers on the pulse of the local market and they focus on the needs of their customers. The customer wants a no-hassle ordering experience, short lines, a full menu that is easy to understand, plenty of parking, plenty of seating, just enough service that they don't have to stand around to wait for their order, and a clean, well-lighted place where they can get some work done. Beans surveys their customers quarterly to determine what they want. They do this with "Buy One Coffee Get One Free" offers when a customer completes a survey. The surveys are held randomly, so the customers do not take advantage of the offer by completing the survey more than once per quarter.

Beans carefully tracks the results of each location. They know the average number of customers that visit each location each day (300), the average ticket per customer ($7.50), the busiest times of the day in each location (7:00 am to 10:30 am), and the top-selling items at each location (coffee of the day). They track their advertising and retain careful records of any coupons or special offers. Their two-for-one coffee offers are always very popular.

Two years ago, Beans started a Coffee Club program within all of its locations. They currently have 3,400 people in their coffee club program, where every 10th cup of coffee is free. This program is tracked carefully by its point of sale system and automatically provides the free cup of coffee simply by swiping the customer's coffee card, without the customer needing to track it. The Coffee Club card operates like a credit card, and helps track the individual purchases of each customer. When the cards are used by the customers, they automatically update the customer database, so the Beans staff knows what items are selling, the average number of visits per week by customer, and the average sales per customer for their Coffee Club members compared to non-members. Beans retains the contact information for every club member, including the mailing address and e-mail address. They use this information to promote their special events, provide special offers, and market their catering business. They also survey their Coffee Club customers once a quarter with a simple e-campaign offer, "Buy One Coffee Get One Free" when a survey is completed. Beans tracks the resulting data very carefully.

II. Objectives:

Katie Smith recently decided to meet monthly with the store managers and company owners to set new objectives for each month. While she still has annual objectives, she decided that involving the store managers in the decision making process, adding a friendly spirit of competition, and increasing the sense of urgency for accomplishing their corporate goals on a location-by-location basis was the best way to move the needle. The monthly and annual objectives follow:

- Current Annual Sales at $5,800,000.
  Objective is to reach $7,000,000 by Year End.

- Current Average Sales per location of $834,000
  Objective is to reach $1,000,000 by Year End.

- Current Average Ticket per Customer of $7.50
  Objective is to reach an Average Ticket per Customer of $8.50 by Year End

- Current Average Number of Customers per Day is 300
  Objective is to reach an Average of 315 Customers per Day

- Currently have 3,400 people in the Beans Coffee Club
  Objective is to have 5,000 people in the Beans Coffee Club by Year End

- Current Catering Business averages $24,000 per Year per Location
  Objective is to increase Catering to an average of $50,000 per Year Per Location

- Current Staff is Friendly, until the locations become very busy, then they switch to survival mode.
  Objective: Friendly Staff All of the Time

III. Strategies:

To attain these Objectives, Katie Smith, the owners, and her team of managers developed the following Strategies:

- Increase Average Ticket Per Customer by Implementing a Cross-Selling Program.

- Increase Average Customers per Day by Marketing to Current Non-Customers Living Within a Two-Mile Radius of Each Location, Distributing Bounce-Back Coupons to Return at Slower Times of the Week, and Offering More Specials to Coffee Club Members.

- Increase the Catering Business by promoting catering sales actively from within each location, promoting it to Coffee Club Members, and marketing to consumers and businesses within a two-mile radius of each location.

- Develop a Customer Service Program that ensures Friendly Staff all of the Time.

- Develop an Employee Incentive Program that Implements the Strategies and Drives Results to Reach the Objectives.

VI. Tactics:

After they completed the company Objectives and Strategies, Katie wrote a Classic 5 Step Marketing Plan for the new year, where she wrote a Situational Analysis for Beans, organized the new corporate Objectives, and summarized the new Strategies. With these first three steps completed, Katie worked with the owners and the store managers to create the Tactics for the year in Step 4. The tactics continued to evolve at the monthly management meetings, until the following final list of tactics was created:

Tactic One: The Daily Phrase. Develop a list of phrases that are designed to cross-sell items at the point of transaction with every customer. For example, when a customer buys a cup of coffee, simply ask "Do you need a power bar now for more power later?" A list of 10 cross-selling phrases will be memorized by each employee to use in different transactional situations with each customer. Employee results will be rewarded in the Employee Incentive Program.
Budget: $00   **Completion Date:** January 15th

Tactic Two: Design and print 7 versions of Bounce-Back coupons to bring customers back during slower times of the day and promote other items; for example, "Smooth Move... Visit us between 1:00 pm and 4:00 pm this week for Cool Deals on Delicious Smoothies. Save $1.50 with this Coupon." Develop instructions for employees for when to pass out each coupon.
Budget: $1,500   **Completion Date:** December 30th

Tactic Three: Design and implement a monthly Direct Mail Campaign that reaches the homes of 5,000 target customers within a 2-mile radius of each location, for a total mailing of 35,000 homes per month. Direct Mail pieces will include bar coded coupons that will be tracked by the point-of-sale register system, to determine which coupon offers work best and that links the coupon to each mailing. Employees must swipe the coupon bar code on the register in order to honor the coupon. Eight different coupon offers will be evaluated throughout the year to determine which coupons are most popular. Additionally, the transaction amounts resulting from each coupon will be carefully tracked to determine the total sales attributed to each direct mail campaign and the highest resulting sales for each coupon. These mailing will be to "non-customers" and current Beans Coffee Club Members will be eliminated. All locations will be listed on each direct mail piece. Beans Catering Services will be mentioned in a special section on every direct mail piece. All direct mail pieces for the year will be printed in one print run for the best price.

Design of 12 Direct Mail Pieces: $2,000
Printing of 420,000 Direct Mail Pieces (35,000 X 12 Mailings): $23,000
Mailing Services and Postage: $105,000
Total Budget: $130,000

Tactic Four: Every customer that brings in a direct mail coupon will be a new customer. Each time a coupon is redeemed, the employee will hand the customer a flyer with details on how to sign up for the Beans Coffee Club. A short sign up form will be on the back of every Coffee Club flyer. Customers will also be able to sign up online. A set of flyers will be delivered to each catered event for the people attending.

Printing 15,000 Coffee Club Flyers: $800   **Completion Date:** December 30th

Tactic Five: Send monthly E-Campaigns to members of the Beans Coffee Club with special offers and inside information on Beans. Design and implement an online template so the monthly content can be added quickly and easily. Develop a calendar of special offers that are tied to holidays and special events. Repeat the offers one week later via Twitter, and a week after that via Facebook, so each offer will be distributed to Coffee Club members 3 times per month, through three different online outreaches. Beans Catering Services will be mentioned in a special section on every E-Campaign. Open rates, click-thrus and links to a special landing page will track responses. Monthly E-mails can be sent at no charge, template creation is the only cost.

Budget: $2,000   **Completion Date:** January 15th

Tactic Six: Beans Catering Services will be promoted within each location with point of purchase displays, table tops, and tri-fold brochures. Employees will pass out flyers to customers who appear to be potential catering clients.

POP Displays: $750   **Completion Date:** December 15th
Table Tents: $650
Tri-Fold Brochures: $1,000
Total Budget: $2,400

Tactic Seven: Redesign website to include Beans Coffee Club page, Catering Services page, and landing pages for the e-Campaigns and the Direct Mail campaign. Include intranet site so employees can login to see Employee Incentive Program results.

Budget: $2,500   **Completion Date:** January 30th

Tactic Eight: Develop a customer service program called "Always Smiling" where the employees greet each customer with a smile and a kind greeting, remembering names when possible. A mystery shopper will be hired to visit the locations and evaluate customer service. Employees will receive rankings that will be factored into the Employee Incentive Bonus Program.
Budget: $4,000   **Implementation:** March 1 – May 31

Tactic Nine: Develop a comprehensive Employee Incentive Program that tracks average ticket per customer, "Always Smiling" performance results, catering sales by location, Beans Coffee Club memberships by location, and bounce-back coupon sales by location. Locations will compete in each of these categories and employees will receive monthly, quarterly and annual bonuses based on store and individual results. Each employee will have a cash register code, so transactions and the resulting metrics are linked to the specific employee. Results will be shared with all employees at monthly meetings and posted on the employee Intranet site. Top employees will receive awards and cash bonuses.
Budget for Bonuses: $30,000   **Completion Date:** On-Going
Budget for Awards: $1,500
Total Budget: $31,500

Total "Actual" Marketing Budget: $174,700
Total "Reserved" Marketing Budget: $175,000

V. Assessment:

Katie Smith will assess the success and results of each of the marketing strategies and tactics by compiling the metrics needed to see if the Beans employee team has accomplished their company objectives. Katie will leverage the technology within their sophisticated point-of-sale register system to track each of the key metrics:

- Total Company Sales / Sales by Location
- Average Ticket per Customer / Average Ticket by Location / by Employee
- Average Customers per Day / By Location
- Mystery Shopper Results
- Number of Coffee Club Memberships
- Total Catering Sales / Total Catering Sales by Location
- Coupons Redeemed / Ranking Top Performing Coupons
- Sales Generated by Redeemed Coupons
- Website and Landing Page Hits / E-Campaign Click-Thrus
- Coffee Club Membership Related Sales

Marketing Dashboard: Katie Smith will develop a marketing dashboard to graphically illustrate and track the success of her marketing programs, the key metrics, employee incentive program results, and the data that will be used in her assessment.

Optimizing the Marketing Matrix: Beans currently has a marketing matrix that includes 4 key tactics: (1) Coffee Club, (2) Direct Mail, (3) Cross-Selling Programs, and (4) E-Campaigns to Coffee Club Members.

Katie is testing the following new programs: (1) Daily Phrase, (2) Mystery Shopper "Always Smiling Program", (3) Bounce-Back Coupons, (4) Catering Sales, and (5) Employee Incentive Program. Katie will carefully evaluate their results compared with last year, and track the important metrics to determine which of these new tactics will remain.

Corporate Brand: Katie will continue to use the same proven corporate branding strategy that has been in place for several years, while featuring the Beans Catering Services within all messaging and campaigns. She will continue to use consistent messaging, images, design, and colors throughout her direct mail, website, e-Campaigns, POP, bounce-back coupons and other tactics.

Additional Items: Katie has a tight budget and will negotiate her purchases carefully.

Katie Smith has used Formula Marketing effectively to align the Beans corporate marketing plan to its objectives. While every tactic may not succeed, Katie will have the ability to track all of their results and quickly determine what changes are needed for the next year. In summary, Katie Smith will know if her marketing formula was a success and why. Over time, she will build a formula that works and generates reliable, predictable results. Her marketing expenditures will reflect carefully planned investments rather than a series of random expenses. Katie will have a proven marketing formula.

CHAPTER 19:
WRITE YOUR MARKETING FORMULA

Now it's time for you to write your Marketing Formula. Follow the steps in the examples within Chapters 16, 17, and 18.

Be sure that your Tactics are aligned with your Situational Analysis, Objectives, Strategies and Assessment. Develop your Marketing Matrix. Make sure each of your marketing Tactics work in concert with one another and synergize them to save money, time and work.

Begin with the notes section on the pages below and craft a Marketing Formula that will define your customers, provide metrics, and guarantee a healthy return on your investment.

I want to wish you great blessings and every possible success in your business endeavors.

Marketing Notes:

David Wilkey

Marketing Notes:

Marketing Notes:

David Wilkey

Marketing Notes:

Marketing Notes:

David Wilkey

Marketing Notes:

Marketing Notes:

David Wilkey

ABOUT THE AUTHOR:

David Wilkey has been a marketing student for over 25 years. He has served as a senior marketing executive for a diverse group of companies, has owned a direct mail advertising company, and has several years of hands-on experience in implementing marketing campaigns for nationally recognized brands. His marketing studies began at the University of Southern California and continue today as a senior marketing consultant for Cordius Group, a commercial print and marketing company. Wilkey is also the owner of InSource Consulting, a marketing consulting firm, and NewSource Communications, an Internet social networking company.